MW00772511

THE CELL BLOCK PRESENTS...

PIMPOLOGY
THE 7 ISMS OF THE GAME

Published by: The Cell Block™

The Cell Block
P.O. Box 1025
Rancho Cordova, CA 95741

Website: thecellblock.net
Facebook/thecellblock.net
Instagram: @mikeenemigo
Corrlinks: info@thecellblock.net

Cover Design: Mike Enemigo

Send comments, reviews, interview and
business inquiries to: info@thecellblock.net

PIMPOLOGY PLAYLIST

Pimpology, by Too $hort

Like a Pimp, by David Banner

Pimpin' Pay Good, by Bankroll Jones

Unthinkable, by Alicia Keys

Gigolos Get Lonely Too, by Morris Day

Hoes, by Too $hort

Choose Up, by Pimpin Tre

Something You Should Know, by Dubee aka Sugawolf

Mr. Wrong, by Mary J. Blige

Born to Mack, by Too $hort

Stayin' on My Toes, by Mac Dre

Juvenile On Fire, by Juvenile

Ain't No Way, by King Ko$a

Game Spittin, by Dubee aka Sugawolf

What These Bitches Want, by DMX

INTRODUCTION

Deep down in the trenches, or far out in the field, wherever the Game gets played, each player possesses his own particular style. In the pimp Game, these individual styles are like a signature. This is what many will refer to as their "Ism" – a slick way of letting it be known that pimp points of view are being discussed.

Just like water, the Game must follow the path of least resistance. There are some that are resistant when they hear the word "pimp" or "pimpin'," so this collection of information is on some Ism. Ism is an energy source that goes deeper in its meaning as the stages of its use becomes more advanced. It evolves in a way that represents an individual's outlook, as well as his insight.

To peep a player's Ism is to understand how he connects his pimpish ways with the living of his everyday life. And the more ways he has of making this connection, the stronger his Ism will be recognized to be. This is why what you do will never be as important as *how* or *why* you do it. You see, there is strength in numbers, so the more ways you know how to play, the stronger your Game will be.

With that said, I'll submit a philosophy that I employ. I believe in the power of Ism because I feel that, when it's real, it can remove any limit on the number of ways it might come to be. The reason for this is because, once you get the basics down, your overall understanding will reveal countless ways to apply it.

In this script, my aim is to narrow our focus down to a few of those basic principles. And since for most people seven is a favorite or significant number, and because it's the seventh letter of the alphabet, which is the letter "G," for Game, let's count out the seven most foundational principles that any player's Ism should be based on. We're going to focus on the seven Isms of the Game.

Throughout the reading of this script, the reader must remember the bonus lesson of Game itself. Because without having any Game about yourself, the doors to applying Ism in any way will remain locked.

Therefore, we will begin with Game...

Many people have been wise enough to see that the Game of chess is a lot like the Game of life. But if you look closely at this fact, you'll realize that it doesn't stop there. Chess is only one of the games that get compared to life. There are many games with many rules that get a comparison to life.

This brings to mind an old-school card Game called "Coon Can." The old men who taught it to me used to say that, 'some coons can, and some coons can't.' They were referring to the breakdown on all the ways the Game had of making cards fit with each other in order to win the Game.

The goal of the Game was to use up all the cards in your hand before the other guy used all the cards in his. A deck of cards has fifty-two cards in it, and these old heads used to always say that you gotta know all fifty-two switches to get good at this Game.

To me, that means that there is a trick for every card in the deck. And once you learn these tricks, you know the

Game well enough to win no matter what kind of hand you're dealt.

This relates to life by showing how experience reveals the many forms of potential success, or failure. And that experience represents Game.

The more Game a player has about himself, the more ability he has to use what comes to him as a way of achieving victory. This includes each principle of "Ism" life may ever lead him to discover.

Imagine that...

HYPNOTISM

"Ain't nothin' to it but to do it."
– Famous Street Saying

I'll start with Hypnotism as the first principle of Ism because it branches off naturally from the bonus lesson of Game.

To process or apply Game on an ever-evolving basis, you'll need to be focused at all times. And the only way to do this is to program your mind to do so. Remember: You can never control or influence anyone else if you can't first control yourself.

A salesman must believe in his product if he wants to be successful at making customers believe in him. And no good karma comes to anyone who is against everyone they meet. That energy will only ultimately turn against them. So, the first aim of hypnosis is self-hypnosis. The kind in which you convince yourself to love all of what you do.

In time, this love will extend into the need to shape your "you" into what is worthy of this love. You'll find ways to justify the belief that your wrongs can be right, and your rights are the most undeniable thing in the world.

The key to hypnosis is suggestion. It's like planting a seed in a garden. The more seeds you plant, the more your garden will grow. So, the more you suggest something, the more the mind will make it so!

Constant suggestions that your mission is a good and worthwhile one will make you shape some part of your reality into fitting that claim. Therefore, any player who wants to win at whatever Game he plays, will learn to be able to say he's playing the right way for the right reasons. And in time, that player's actions will reflect those thoughts.

This removes the chance of any kind of guilt or other distraction that doesn't line up with the goal of pimpin'. And that's important for avoiding the flood of things that can go wrong in life.

The streets are full of bums, dope fiends, and has-been types who never make it in the long run because they never mastered the art of loving themselves. Either you will take control of your mind, or you're leaving the door open for other things to come along and control you. Next thing you know, you've lost control of your outcome in life, too, and you're lost.

I remember back when I was real young, I used to see the grown men around me hustling, but I never wondered about anything except the nice things these players had. So, when I got old enough to get in the Game myself, all I had in mind to go on was to what really amounts to the temptation.

If you put a carrot in front of a donkey, you can make it move in whatever direction you want, because it'll follow that carrot. And for a few years, I was that jackass who followed the carrot of material things into all kinds of trouble.

Until I learned that I needed to get a grip on my own mind, I was spinning my wheels. In a deadly arena, that means I was out there jeopardizing my life for no reason.

This left the door open for me to get into the bullshit long before I ever got into the real shit. Drinking every day led to smoking weed all day, and then to tooting coke here and there. At first a little, then a lot.

Next in line was an association with gunslingers and the gunplay that comes with that crowd. Because of this, I was a million miles away from being a big baller with nice things. Somehow, I'd slipped into being just another wild-ass young dummy wasting my life in the streets. Robbery and small-time drug dealing bought me a couple of raggedy cars and a few pieces of cheap swap-meet jewelry. That helped me to dabble with prostitutes because they came my way here and there.

Nothing lasted, though, and by the time I found myself on my way to prison at 18 years old, all I had to show for four years on being in the Game was a gold chain and a pistol-grip shotgun.

It was during that trip to prison that I finally got the chance to get a grip on my own mind, because it gave me time away from the Game to organize all the information I'd picked up along the way.

The first lesson was in the form of finding out how much respect people had for me. I was surprised to see that people had heard of me, and real niggas saw me as a real nigga too. I knew I wasn't no sucka, but I thought I'd have to prove this. I wasn't aware of the fact that I had already let that be known before I got to prison. My street record was official. And being left with no choice other than being honest with myself, I realized that many of the mistakes I'd made were because I didn't know this.

I did not yet have the habit of seriously communicating with myself. But I eventually recognized that most of the more notorious and legendary people I got close to spent more time communicating with themselves than anyone else. I learned that everyone worth paying attention to had first paid attention to themselves to know they wasn't just another face in the ghetto. And in knowing this, they convinced themselves that they had to do and be more than average.

That's when the dedicated pimp part of me came to be. Because even though I was known in dope dealing and gunplay circles, I was known for having hoes around me. When I got to Folsom State Prison, I wasn't noticed for stabbing people and fighting. I was noticed for being in that visiting room with a bad bitch every weekend.

I began to recognize about myself what a concentration of the realest people I've ever known recognize about me. Now it wasn't just enough to want nice things, I needed nice things to let it be known that I was about my money on some player shit. And I needed to be about my money to keep away from the bullshit I'd gotten into up to that point.

I was already a hustler who got money, so now I just needed to make better choices with my money moves, because I needed to be the best choice a woman could make. How else could I get them to pay me instead of some clown with a drug habit? I needed to zoom in on this hustle to push the other shit that landed me in prison out of my life. I couldn't just be out there playin' with it to look cute.

The list went on and on, but it was now a list of needs, not just wants. I began to take shit more seriously, and it all grew into reasons and ways to grow into being a better hustler.

I began to compare myself to other notable hustlers and was honest about what they had that I was lacking. That made me want to improve myself even more, because any woman willing to sacrifice herself to put her man in peak position deserves proper satisfaction. And I needed to be that man who was worth such an effort and investment.

My mind went back to my first dealings with hoes so many times that I knew there were points I was meant to recognize – lessons I needed to learn that were important to my life. I wasn't yet aware of how the bonus lesson of Game itself could unlock the doors that separated the ways that Ism could be applied, so the connecting of my lessons was yet to be achieved.

I learned the long way. There were no shortcuts for me. I got my lessons one at a time, even if they came quickly, one after another.

That is, until I started to fantasize about my future and remember my past, all at the same time. That's when I saw with clarity that I was yet to ever give a woman what I wanted women to have from me in times to come.

At that point, I understood why my main bitch was gone so soon after my arrest. She couldn't stick around when I'd given her nothing to stick to. I was actually lucky that she didn't bounce *before* I went to jail.

I chewed on the bitter taste of that self-reflection for a long time. It fueled me into improving, because I didn't want to repeat embarrassing mistakes that landed my main folks surviving on their own in the jungle of the Bay with no tools at all.

The kind of company I kept came to make much more of a difference. Being from the Bay Area, where even the stone-cold killers come across in a slick kind of playeristic way, made me careful. I was used to hanging out with killers, but that habit caused me to be sidetracked.

Even though most of the people I knew could pass scrutiny and be considered real individuals, that same level of scrutiny revealed a lot of what I didn't want to be. Robbery and murder is not player shit. Just like sellin' dope while fuckin' every bitch you meet is not pimpin'.

Sometimes, for some people, the first step towards loving yourself is to hate yourself. Love should make life better, so if you love yourself too much, you'll never improve upon who and how you are as a person.

I cleared my mind of all the things I disliked about myself through constant suggestion that none of those things were really me. It was a lonely time in life because I started keeping to myself. And not too long after that, I was transferred to Susanville.

In Susanville I ran into an old player who I knew from seeing with my own eyes was a 100 percent real pimp. His name is Diamond. He's from Richmond, like me, so I had seen him on the track many times around town, as well as all over the Bay Area, like Oakland and San Francisco.

Diamond also had a baby by one of my main buddy's auntie, so I'd bumped into him on a more family kind of level, too. And besides mine, recognizing a face was something he wasn't able to do with anyone else on that prison yard. Therefore, we got pretty close for almost a year before he got out.

I don't know if he hypnotized me, or coached me into subconsciously hypnotizing myself. Maybe it was a little bit of both. All I know for sure is that, through our daily conversations, I learned a lot. Every pimp worth mentioning in the Bay Area at that time became my teacher through Diamond's stories.

And it wasn't gossip, either. Each story was told as an example of some point he was trying to make. He rarely answered my questions directly. What he did instead was tell me something about someone in a way that showed the answer to whatever I was asking.

Being down and around enough to know the people he was speaking about brought these stories to life. I was able to envision each situation in vivid detail, and identify with every success, each failure, and all the corrections to those failures. It had the effect of personal experience! So, when Filmore Slim told Diamond the secret to how pimps remain successful, I may as well have been in the back seat overhearing it.

This is how I learned how to keep it official and authentic; because Dinky told Tone Mac that his clean-ass car needed to come from ho money to be a pimp trophy.

When Stiffy the Pimp bought ol' girl a Corvette and she ran off with it, I learned to be careful who I fucks with, and not to do too much, too soon.

The Downs brothers from West Oakland taught me not to lose myself in drug abuse, and that everything that glitters ain't gold.

Kenny Red and Gangster Brown showed me how dedication is a must. And even at times when it don't look the best, you'll win in the end if you stay down with what you claim to be.

Double R was proof that birds of a feather should flock together, and if you want to be great, you surround yourself with greatness.

Hollyrock taught me the value of having a good measure of gangster ability in the bloodline of a pimp's pedigree, while Mac Slim and Lil Nate balanced it out by proving that I shouldn't depend too much on my pistol play for problem solving.

Pimp James, Pimp Wayne, Crooked-Mouth Pierre, Hook the Crook, Cash Money 'Mont, Easy Money Ed, and many others all taught me that the best ain't only the ones you heard the most about. And that bitch Nikki, aka Super Ho, let me know that one great provider can have a real P living better than he would if he had five good providers. So, count bread, not heads.

Stacking and managing money became an obsession for me. I learned that it was smarter to make payments or save up for one real piece of jewelry than it was to quickly buy up a bunch of junk that ain't worth shit. I was sick when I looked back as how much I'd wasted. And this inspired me to get it all again, if for no other reason than to get it right this time. My mind folded in on itself endlessly about how wrong it would be for me to treat the money a woman gave me in an incorrect way.

Gang members represent the set they claim. In other places, like the Bay Area, we represent the block or turf that we hustle on. This includes projects, apartment complexes, etc. And if a pimp is really what a man claims to be, he will come to represent his Ism with as much passion and pride as all of the above.

The development of my Ism began with this mental journey, taking an honest look at myself and all that I was, up to the point of realizing what I was supposed to be, then adjusting myself accordingly after I compared the two versions.

I put all my conscious energy into applying what I respected most to who I would present myself to be when the world got another look at me. So, when my girlfriend decided to leave me, as most girlfriends will do when a guy goes to prison, I decided she was a waste of my time anyway.

Then that decision graduated into considering a bitch as my girlfriend to be disrespectful in general. How dare I have a girlfriend and expect a ho to pay me? And how dare a ho think she's going to be my girlfriend? Furthermore, how dare a square bitch go and try to be my girlfriend, knowing I'm a pimp?

This all represented a violation against the integrity of my Ism, because girlfriends weren't prostitutes, and I was in hot pursuit for a prostitute as all times.

If hoes bought my cars, clothes, and jewelry, plus paid for my attention, there was no way to justify a girlfriend enjoying any part of my existence for free. I had to stick to the script, and the script I was writing for myself had no room for anything like that. If I wanted anyone to follow my program, I had to follow it, too.

These thoughts became my reality, as all thoughts will. In the field of dreams, the controlling theme comes down to a catchphrase: If you build it. . . they will come.

Well, my mind was the field of my dreams and my thoughts were the seeds. Those thoughts grew into the tree of my Ism as I hypnotized myself into being who I am.

Without having a team, I built myself into a team coach, a team captain, and a team mascot. Through self-hypnosis, I built something of myself that a team would come to, so that wherever I might be, it wouldn't be long before a team came to me.

There is a fact that is so real, it may as well be supported by scientific proof. And that fact is that you will draw to yourself whatever you focus on the most. I proved this to myself after a little while of staying focused on what me and Diamond discussed. After he went home, I was transferred to another prison, closer to the Bay Area. In this new place, there was much more opportunity for me to spread my wings, because I was given the job of being a porter, also often called a tier tender. Basically, I was the janitor for my unit. This assignment landed me outside my cell more than everyone else, so most inmates needed my help to make their moves. Some of these moves included making phone calls for guys who were locked inside their cells, and I enjoyed this hustle the most because it was contraband-free, so no risk was involved.

The bonus was that I got a chance to talk to a lot of females in the free world. And being trustworthy made me the guy people used most for this service. And because of this, some of these women were on the phone with me so often, they felt like they knew me after a while.

What worked most in my favor was that I kept it solid. I never tried to come up on nobody's chick or family member in any way at all. But I did talk me ass off enough to shoot my shots and put myself in the mix. It was just in a way that would help whatever dude I was calling for instead of myself. There were dudes on the yard who couldn't even get their girl to visit or send packages until I started calling these girls for them.

After a while, these girls naturally wondered what was up with their buddy Man-Man who'd been calling all the time. Why isn't he in the visiting room? Does he have a girl? That's when hook-ups started coming my way. These girls wanted me to meet their sisters and cousins and friends. They wanted to see me in the visiting room enjoying myself, too. One or two of these girls even recognized Game enough to know I was a perfect match for one of her peoples who was cute but needed guidance.

Real individuals trusted and respected me enough to have my back. This crossed over to their women, too. And real women want to put a real man in a positive position, so these women steered their real partners in my direction.

Before I knew what was going on, my self-hypnosis had built me into having a selection of ready-made go-getters to choose from. And when the time came for me to go free, I had the first member of my team already contributing to my cause. She came to me as a Christmas gift when no one else I knew came to visit me for the holiday. After I turned her out, I named her Sunshine, and we had a drop-top Mustang three weeks after she started getting down for me.

Sunshine was a tall, thick, slick-ass red bone with green eyes, whose father was a con man and mother was a ho. Together we went from a little bit of nothing to a whole lot of money, but I never would've touched a dime without first convincing myself I should have every penny of what she gave me.

Sunshine didn't live in the Bay at first, so I had to travel to go visit with her. I eventually got a parole violation for being out of my fifty-mile radius.

During my first few months of the four-month violation, she sent me six or seven hundred dollars and a bunch of stamped envelopes to write her. Then she got back with her ex-boyfriend on some sneaky shit, but she stayed in touch with me and was even there to pick me up when I got back out. She never knew I'd heard about the boyfriend. My cell-mate was her cousin's baby daddy, though, so the news was official.

But the pimp in me was official, too. So a boyfriend who never stopped her from being there for me was no threat. As far as I was concerned, she kept it real with me. I was so convinced that she was my ho in training, and I was her pimp in waiting, a boyfriend had nothing to do with what we were into.

This is where the subject crosses over from self-hypnosis into Hypnotism of others. Once you control yourself, you can control your situation. And for a pimp, most situations include hoes.

If you ever see someone get hypnotized on TV or in a movie, certain things are common. First, the person is told to focus on something, then they're told to listen to something. Those are the basic ingredients.

So, in my world, my Ism is the point of all focus. Every detail of it that is visible – cars, clothes, jewelry, other hoes, etc. – are tools. And I use all these tools either make a point, or prove a point that I made some other way, so that somehow everything about my program will stand as a constant example or reference.

For example, a peacock in a park will make me talk about why I'm supposed to have jewelry as a real P. And the tires on a car will make me speak on why any real team needs at least four hoes.

From bullets in a gun to a rabbit on the run; I'll use it all as a reason to give a shout-out to my pimpin'. And I do it tastefully with skill and consideration, so it fits. And in time, this will establish the language of thought within my world. Like a lens of a certain color placed over the eyes so that everything in now that same color.

I remember one time I got a job at a finance company. They re-financed home mortgages for people. But we had to make cold calls to find customers. During training they kept drilling into us how everyone is a potential customer, and the most successful reps make this a lifestyle. They were slick about it, but by the time you got the entire lesson being taught, you were aware that you were being asked to be at work everywhere you go. At all times you were supposed to be looking for customers.

Then, around the office, you could literally not have a single communication with the senior staff without the subject of "closing a deal" coming up. It was like a religious culture of salesmanship around the place. And I must admit, it got results.

I also have some cousins down in Compton, California who live in a well-known hood, so of course, as we got older, the whole gang bangin' thing became a part of my big cuzzo's life. What was crazy to me was how his homeboys could listen to any song and ad-lib the words into being all about their gang and their hood. I mean, niggas who don't even rap or sing, doin' it off the top of their head without missin' a beat! Not just one song, either. They did it with *every* song. And whenever I smoked with them or rode in the car somewhere, their whole convo was about why the enemies was some bitches, the allies was cool, or some other hood politics.

So, it was no surprise that so many of that generation were willing to die, kill, or do life in prison for what they represented. They ate, slept, and breathed that shit daily, with no days off!

These niggas were hypnotized into a frame of seeing life where everything was one color, most words started with one letter, their street was the one number they mentioned most, and the name of their gang was the most powerful word imaginable. Nothing good, or strong, or desirable was described or talked about without attaching "Nutty" to it.

I respected it, but it wasn't for me. I'm a Bay boy, through and through. But I did learn one valuable lesson from them, though: Make sure whatever your walk is about, it's reinforced by what you talk about. That's how you get and keep people on your hype.

I respect Bishop Don Juan immensely for a lot of reasons, but one of the slickest moves he made was to choose the colors green and gold and run with it how he did. I can't honestly claim to know what's behind the whole green and gold thing besides green being for the money and gold being for the honey, but I do know that in this Game, when you see those colors, you think of him. And that's a form of hypnosis.

By constantly connecting his image to those colors, that man taught the world to think about him. And he did it in a way that goes beyond any mental safeguards one might have in place.

So, when we look at all of that, we know how useful and powerful hypnotism can be. Is there any way anyone should leave this out of their program?

I would go as far as to say that if Realism is what a pimp's final destination should be, then Hypnotism is what his final product should be. The things you do should always be in pursuit of those two Isms. All else is done in observance of the other individual principles.

Anything less is leaving the door open for some other point of focus to edge its way into the mind of your teammate's and steal the show away from you. If that happens, you won't be far from having your team stolen from you as well. That's why commercials come on over and over again throughout the day. The companies know they can hypnotize you into wanting their product if you see and hear about it enough.

When you tryna pimp, you're your own commercial. And the repetitive references to your Ism is what keeps your Game tight, because you want everybody involved in your mix to be aiming the energy of their focus towards your Game.

SOCIALISM

"A mad move is a bad move."
– Pimp Proverb

Whenever I hear the word "socialist," it's being used in the same way as "capitalist" or "communist." Like, to describe the political style a particular group or country bases their views on. That's why I love the concept behind the word "context." Because it opens the door for one thing to mean many things, depending on how you apply it.

My application of the word Socialism doesn't have a damn thing to do with any political view, even though it could be said that it's a guideline on how to politic with your pimp program.

Socializing with a social consciousness aimed toward a successful outcome, that's what I'm on with this particular principle. Success should be the goal in anything anybody does. And all social interaction should involve other people. So, the "Socialism" we're trying to employ is based on trying to socialize successfully with your folks.

Since success leads to happiness in most cases, any real successful social situation should leave all parties involved feeling happy about their involvement. The social aspect of your Ism is made up of caring about how you affect the people you deal with, because it's a must to make them happy in some kind of way.

Men should not be out to dog as many women as possible. And women should not be out to trip up as many men as they can. Impressing friends and making useless points should be the last thing on anyone's agenda. Like, not on the agenda at all. That's how a lot of people lose in the Game of life; they stay focused on the wrong things and get off track.

It's also why so many women are closed to the idea of their men having other women on his team – because Socialism was never applied whenever the subject of multiple women was brought to the table.

You can't be shy in the Game, but that doesn't mean you're supposed to be a social butterfly, either, that's for sure!

A woman who knows me won't immediately tell herself that I'm chasing pussy or going on dates if she hears about me in connection to another woman. If you put me in a room full of people, I might not speak to a single person. But if you surround me with a bunch of good hoes that all gave me stacks, I'll be doing all I can to make sure everybody is good. Because if that group of women look like they made a bad decision in choosin' me, then I look bad. Just like they look stupid sayin' they get money if I'm lookin' like I'm hurtin' for money. We represent each other in a way that should make each other's image just as important as our own image is to us.

That's called sharing the same vision. And your social circle should all share the same vision.

Nobody can ever walk anywhere if their legs are busy going in opposite directions. They would look real stupid and probably fall on their ass. A team is one body, and they must all be on the same page. A house divided against itself cannot stand. There's no way around that.

But drama is so popular these days, a lot of people think that's what life is about. It's like a person isn't considered strong if they're not a fighter. So now you got the whole country full of shit starters who can't get along with each other. And nobody has the sense enough to stand up for the fact that it still takes teamwork to make the dream work.

A healthy level of being competitive is OK. But jealousy is a cancer that should never ever be seen as anything to be proud of. It will lead to a team playing against each other. And once that starts, you may as well start over since that group is a done deal.

This can be avoided by maintaining social awareness in your Ism. Don't leave anyone out when it comes to promoting smiles. And check yourself enough to know if your moves are good for your team or not.

I remember the very first time I had more than one member on my team. We all lived in the same house with my main bitch's mother. Me and my number one were still young, but her mother was a well-known vet in the Game who had been a ho for over ten years already.

By the time I got up to having three go-getters on my squad, the mama was givin' my bitches more guidance than I was. But she liked me, though, so she gave me a lot of Game, too. And she never played against me, so I had to respect her.

Everything was good until I got that third member on my team. Being only 17 at the time, I was still too green to know that more bitches could mean more problems if I wasn't careful to accept only good ones, and that third one was a crafty one who I should've never let into my business. She was a few years older than me, so she thought she could run the show.

At the time, my number one was the only one gettin' any kind of sex play from me, but number three saw that as a kind of trophy she wanted since number two wasn't gettin' it. She got more money than number two and got along with number one, so eventually she worked her way into my presence a lot more than she should've been allowed to.

Somehow, she figured out that number one was gettin' the goods whenever I'd come home drunk. And she was so slick, she knew she could get it by suggesting a threesome. My number one was so down for whatever, she thought I would like that she jumped on it. So, one night they got me tipsy off the gin and ambushed my pimpin'. Nobody knew how much this hurt my number two except Mama Linda, who sat with her while she cried about being left out. And even though I made it up to her once it was brought to my attention, the vibe never got back to 100 percent official.

Because my number three had a separate aim and the stage was set, her poison infected the rest of my program like a virus, and I wasn't ready for that. For a long time after that experience, I wondered how I should've protected myself better. But after a while of collecting more experience and having a few key conversations, I can to realize it was my team that I should've been protecting, not myself. They depended on me to have their back and represent our dream. Nothing new should've been able to come along and fuck off our flow. That third bitch was accepted because I was trusted. And it was on me to keep it solid enough that she would/should have known her place. Also, she should never have been able to be so close so quick without proving she was worthy.

The roads we travel in life are never as important as our reasons for choosing those particular roads, and each member of your team should be an important part of that reason. This is the social consideration that should exist somewhere in your Ism. Because it's not only you out there. Your hoes are in it to win it, too.

I had to have this lesson come at me in a few different ways before I got a full understanding of it. At first, I tried to narrow it down to remembering to always do "this," or never allowing anyone to do "that." But it's not about "this" or "that." It's about the "who," the "what," and the "why." *Who* are you down with? *What* do you stand for, and *why* is this what you're doing? Those are the real questions.

Dream big and sell your dream at the highest price you can. Then dedicate yourself to giving your investors what they paid for. This should be what carries more weight than anything else that doesn't fit itself into this specific equation.

Once the full understanding of this point became a part of my everyday Ism, I noticed a big increase in how far my Ism could take me. It got to the point where, even when I was between hoes, I spent my alone time working on my image, so any woman who got with me could be proud to point me or my car out to other bitches on the block.

By adding social concerns to my Ism, I added reasons to my list of motivation. Increased motivation improved performance, and that gave better overall results. My team grew when the members knew I was on a mission to stick to the script. There's not a ho on earth who's gonna welcome a new member to her team just so her folks can fuck off.

So if you don't rock with who's rollin' for you, your program will be stuck on stupid for sure. It won't ever get any bigger or better. That isn't only bad business, it's sad business. And it's also the reason why renegades are out there so deep these days – because they can't be sure they will get what they want out of playing their position in the Game with a pimp. On top of that, a lot of these new-age hoes had a bad introduction to the Game, so they act and operate in ways that go against what a proper program would provide.

I've noticed a growing trend in the media towards turning people against each other. Everybody is portrayed as some kind of person you need to defend against, and everything is some kind of scam now.

Trust is being put out there like it's some sort of weakness that leads to being victimized. And communication is always conflict or confrontation, otherwise it has no entertainment value.

Bullshit is the new reality these days. That's why all the "reality" shows teach us that drama is real life now. And the people who follow these wacked-out examples don't even know they're being hypnotized into going nowhere in life, so they run around in aimless circles, starting over again and again after every weekend relationship.

We have to pick our folks and stick with them to build. When any group of two or more agree on something and pursue it daily, they get it. That positive aim of energy is the closest thing to magic anybody will ever see.

Any Ism that doesn't observe this won't last long.

What I like to do the most in observance of this principle is teach my team how to love money as much as I do. At this point, the lesson overlaps with Realism and Hypnotism, because this aspect of Socialism consists of spoiling your ho from time to time. That way she's happy she gave you the damn money. How you do it is up to you, as long as you do it in some kind of way.

Loving what money makes possible is a one-way ticket to loving money. And loving money is a strong motive to make a person want to get money.

This blends into Realism by covering the requirement of providing real results for your team. And it blends into Hypnotism by adding strength to the suggestion that paying you is a good thing for a ho to do. So how can you lose by developing a habit like this?

Real dope is gonna get you high no matter how you get it into your system, right? Because those chemicals will have the affect no matter what. And in the same scenario, real Ism is gonna keep you pimpin' no matter how it fits into your Game, because the principles will have the desired affect no matter what.

With that being said, let's get back onto the subject of spoiling hoes for social purposes. You're treating your team how you would treat yourself. And that makes it more than just talk when you say that they represent you. Because when you see them, you see extensions of yourself, and how you treat them proves this. So, if you're making sure your clothes, shoes, car, etc. is on point, I can promise you it'll be even more so if you make sure your team can say the same about themselves. Therefore, if a woman pays you correctly, you should spoil her correctly. Consider it your re-up money. You gotta spend it to make it, ya dig?

One time I had a wild little youngsta out of Kentucky who liked to play with her nose. But I was done with the blow by then, so when her twenty-first birthday came, I didn't get her any powder to toot on. She was mad, but she didn't speak on it, because what I did do was burn through more than two stacks that day to make sure she was happy. I rented her a limo and rode her all around the safe parts of Washington, D.C. I bought her some diamond earrings and took her shopping on an Air Jordan and True Religion extravaganza. I got her a room at the Ritz Carlton in Georgetown for enough money nightly to pay rent monthly at an apartment in Las Vegas. I also got her an ounce of the best weed to smoke however she wanted (at east coast prices), and big bottles of that hundred-dollar Moet Rose champagne. I got her dinner in the restaurant at the lobby in the Ritz, plus we went crazy on room service.

But no coke...

So, I'm thinkin' I hit a real homerun with the bitch, and I felt she deserved it because she had given me around $13,000 over the past two weeks.   But I never considered how much she wanted to toot some blow. Or maybe I just didn't know. She hadn't been fuckin' with any since she'd been with me. I'm guessing that was her thing before I knocked her, though, because when we got back to business a couple days later, I woke up to find the bitch was gone. She'd taken some money and caught a bus back to Kentucky on me.

As I'm sitting there in a hotel in Virginia, I'm wondering two things: One, how could this ho do me like this after I just blessed her? And two, why didn't this ho take all the money? She'd left me still holding almost ten bands!

As I was trying to figure it all out, I got a text from the little silly muthafucka sayin' she was sorry. At this point, there was nothin' left for me to do except try and get myself a ho, so that's what I did; I got that ho back on my team!

When she returned, I didn't beat her up. I gave her a hug and called her stupid, because one of the promises I made to bring her back was to not smash her for runnin' off like that. I had to ask her two questions, though. First one was why on earth she would take the chance on coming back. And the other was why didn't she take all the money when she left.

She told me that the way I spoiled her made her want to see me with that money. And she came back because she knew that was the best birthday of her entire life, and she didn't want me to regret doing it for her like that.

I won't lie, I felt like she was saying what she thought I wanted to hear. But do you honestly think any part of that scenario would've worked in my favor had I not ever spoiled that bitch? Think about it.

And even though I gave that ho a pass on kickin' her ass, she was right back to work the same hour she got back to me. This would not have been possible if I would've done what some would think she rightfully deserved. Plus, by the next day, she had replaced what she took anyway.

She made close to a thousand dollars a day for me, every single day, for months after that. I got mad at her and blew all the bread and she made it right back. That was her punishment.

Then she went on to buy me my first Mercedes-Benz. And I was nowhere near broke after I bought it. I would say Socialism being properly applied to my Ism served me very well. But it never would've benefitted me if I had not allowed it to benefit ol' girl, too. You can't keep someone else down without keeping yourself from coming up as well.

In the process of keepin' it pimpin', you must pimp past or through some things from time to time, because that will be what it takes to keep the pimp shit going on. Otherwise, it will turn from pimp shit to some whole other kind of shit.

Socialism consists, at times, of putting yourself in someone else's shoes. Understand what someone besides yourself may be thinking or feeling. I won't lie, this is often hard for me to do, but then my Realism allows me to at least see why they might think or feel a certain way, and that bridges the gap. Shit, how else is the money supposed to cross over from them to me? I'm there to get paid; not argue, debate, beg, or fight. So, who I'm dealing with is going to have to get their way in the process of me getting my way.

There's always another way you can satisfy your pride or ego besides it being at your folk's expense. And if it's your anger you're trying to satisfy, you need to pump the breaks anyway, because a mad move is a bad move...

Here's a detailed fact to always remember: A ho may not love herself at the end of the day. She won't always be aware of this fact, but it will still remain to be true. It's a truth that lies dormant deep beneath the surface of who she is or how she thinks.

Because up front, on the surface of her consciousness, is the things she does and the things she wants. There's a possibility that she might judge herself harshly for being a ho. Or maybe she's a ho because she judges herself harshly due to some kind of social stain on her square existence that she ain't proud of.

Whatever the case may be, this can lead that individual into making the kind of fucked up moves that will bring her fucked up results. It's a self-punishment that can reach the extreme of having suicidal tendencies. Usually, though, it'll show itself in the form of some other self-destructive habit. Smoking, drugs, drinking, etc., are all examples of this.

Any living being is going to have an element of self-preservation. Nobody is going to intentionally remain in a harmful or dangerous situation forever. This is why a ho will end up running away from a man who does overly-violent things to her.

But, the other hidden part will also, at the same time, make her do the kind of things that make a man want to harm her. And this don't only apply to hoes, it applies to people in general. So don't let yourself be anybody's tool for destroying themselves. That means you don't just blindly react to what a ho does without thinking first. And this goes all the way from one extreme to the next.

A proper comprehension of this information will help you to sometimes laugh at the things a woman does. And that'll keep you in the Game of gettin' paid.

Because you catch more bees with honey...

This doesn't mean all you'll ever be is sweet, so don't get the shit twisted. It just means that too much of anything (even a good thing) is a bad thing.

I started with what should be your outcome. That's the fulfillment of everyone involved – including, of course, your own success.

I've gone into the consideration aspects and the spoiling maneuver because it's best to do away with the myths and misunderstandings. And yes, let's admit that most people think pimpin' is all about mahsin' for your rations. Going hard on a bitch and being mean is what the average person in or out of the Game thinks the pimp Game is all about.

I started off with the things I know do not fit with common knowledge, but none of that is to say you're supposed to attempt to build your Ism castle on some dumb-ass peace rally pimpin'. There may indeed be times within the process of managing a ho that you need to be physical in the proving of your point. Just like with dealing with other men, or in the raising of children, or even the training of dogs, you may have to use physicality to help emphasize a point or show you're serious.

But understand my statement clearly before you tell yourself that I'm saying pimps should beat their hoes up. I said you *may* need to get physical when emphasizing a point or show you're serious. So, recognize that you also *may not* need to do all that, and if you do, the point is to prove the fact that you're serious; not the fact that you'll prove it.

And getting physical don't necessarily mean beat your woman up, either. You can get physical without laying a hand on her. Or you can lay a hand on her without harming her.

Now, I know the Me-Too movement will condemn me for saying all of this, but I'ma say the rest of it anyway. There are women out there who enjoy getting into the real rough stuff. And there are those out there who are into pushing a man over the edge of that threshold, just to prove they can. But those types usually flip the script when you give them that side of you. Next thing you know, she's a victim, and you're fighting a felony charge.

I suggest that if you can justify being overly-violent toward your woman because of something she does, you should leave that woman. That's a better solution than giving her what she deserves, because you don't deserve what might happen to you after you do "the fool."

Now, I'm not here to say you ain't pimpin' if you hit your hoes. But jail sure does knock a pimp out of the box, so why even entertain the possibility?

And from my own extremely extensive experience, I've learned that the more intelligence I've gathered, the less difficulty I've had with keeping my hands to myself. My personal truth is that, the dumber I was, the more I expressed myself with physical force. And therefore, I won't sit here and tell you to do what I think was stupid.

For that reason, I will say if you can't figure out for yourself some way to do what I'm saying without abusing your woman, keep your hands to yourself. Because my main and only objective in bringing this aspect of Ism up it to make a point. The point is that too much of anything is a bad thing. The constant balance you must maintain is a proper dose of whatever your situation calls for. Never too much of anything, just like never not enough, either. Because coming from the kind of place where nice guys finish last, I still must admit goin' hard wasn't always the answer either.

Remember how tricks get treated and make sure you don't fall into that category. But also remember that your folks are not the enemy. You're on the same team. And sometimes when she fucks somethin' up, she needs your guidance more than your discipline.

Look at whatever she did to make you unhappy. Did she do it on purpose? Did she know better than to do it? Did she show a bad character trait? There's a thin line between disregard and disrespect, but there's still a difference between the two that's worth paying attention to.

And how well do you know her? Was her mama some crash dummy who taught her how to be a crash dummy too? Are there people in her life who steer her in a direction that clashes with what you want? Or, is she just a rotten apple?

All of that and more are the kind of things you need to consider when you're deciding how to react to a bad move on her part. And while you're at it, you need to be real enough to admit to yourself if her mistake is the result of a bad move on your part.

This is how you figure out the recipe on what will make your next move your best move. Because more often than not, you can pimp past most problems.

However, when this is not possible, you can still play your way past it; because sometimes the best way to deal with a problem is to *not* deal with a problem.

In all the *Star Wars* movies, "the force" was what all the Jedi people needed to have control of, because they weren't a Jedi until they could use that force. Well, in the pimp Game, the pimp is like a Jedi, and "the force" is your Ism. So if you trust, depend on, and put your energy into your

Ism, you'll be able to pimp more with the power of your mind. And that'll take you further in the long run.

Socialism is about how many ways you can relate to the woman in your life, not how you can retaliate against her. A lot of times the part you play is decided by the way you set your stage. So, think *pro*-social with your team, not *anti*-social....

SEPARATISM

"A mad move is a bad move."
— Pimp Proverb

Here is yet another term that I've heard used mainly in a limited way that I don't think should define it.

Racist groups are usually also separatist groups that believe interracial mixing should not happen. And I won't waste any time addressing such a silly idea.

Let's just say that my meaning of Separatism is on some whole other shit.

Separatism has a place among the seven principles of Ism, because people involved need to know how to separate one thing from another on many levels, including separating one person from another. And in observing this principle, I would recommend one remember the bonus lesson of using Game itself to maximize the ways in which it can be applied.

As with most things related to Ism, the first part of any point needs to be applied to your own outlook on things. It all starts with your mindset.

Separatism is actually the other part or co-part of Socialism, because when you open your heart and mind to your folks, you should close those same parts of yourself off to anyone outside of that circle. You vibe with your tribe and that's it. Anything else other than family in the off season is outta pocket. And that goes for pimps as much as it goes for hoes.

This philosophy is the reason why prostitutes are supposed to completely ignore any man other than their man unless it's about a hustle. Some people say just ignore other pimps and everyone else is a trick. But I say if a trick ain't talkin' about money, a good ho should ignore his ass too.

And when a pimp's part is being properly played, some form of this same rule applies to him as well. Any woman who has not paid him should not have access to his smile, his sex, or his sweet words. He may stretch these rules to use those tools for convincing a woman to pay him, but I know from experience that you better have an advanced understanding of the Game before you try to get away with this. Bottom line is, some kind of attention must be paid to the process of separating non-team members from team members as a beginning to the application of Separatism as a principle of Ism. It's the only way you can present what you represent as something worthy of respect and recognition. And it also reassures your teammates.

A rival pimp will know your ho has some folks if she ignores him. And if he's playing fair he'll only go so far in his efforts to pull her, because he respects the Game. And outside hoes will know they have to pay you for socializing openly and freely with you if you stay in pocket with them. This should make your folks feel confident that your pimpin' is worthy of respect, so when you do knock another ho, she don't gotta worry about you being on no bullshit with her.

Separatism gives potential participants something to shoot for. Because until they come correct and play their part, they are separate from enjoying your program in any way.

But beware, because it can also give participants a real reason to be offended if you don't carefully observe and consider it in your steps as a pimp.

There's a time that comes to mind when I was doing real good on the east coast. I had a two-girl team and they were both happy, so my flow was one of the best I'd ever had, even though I've had a few good ones.

At first, the principle of Separatism worked in my favor without me even knowing it. Personal moments with each individual just naturally occurred privately. Respect for each other made us responsible with how we operated without any need for pre-planning. And the result was a harmony I wish I wouldn't never taken for granted.

But we all make mistakes. And since very few lessons in the Game will ever come for free, the multiple lessons I learned at once almost cost me everything I owned.

My problem was that my pimpin' was pretty advanced at the time, so I thought my success was based on my skill instead of the true ingredients that went into that recipe. And in feeling myself too much, I slipped from doing it right into doing it wrong. I told myself that my team understood what I wanted without realizing why. So I took their understanding as a given, and I knocked a snowbunny out of Philadelphia. However, when I talked big about flying to Philly to turn me out a new bitch, I didn't sound as good to my team as I did to myself, because the small detail I overlooked was that ol' girl was yet to be turned out. That meant this bitch was not a prostitute. And all my team heard was how I was doing an awful lot to go meet up with a square bitch. And that square bitch had never done even a little bit for our team.

In their minds, the fact that she never paid me should've separated her from being worth any effort on my part. Especially any effort that cost money.

It was my job to be considerate of this outlook, and at the very least, I should have kept my business to myself. But I had yet to learn this lesson. So in my ignorance, I just piled my problems up with one bad move after another.

Once I got to Philly, I stayed in touch with my team thinking I was keepin' shit real about my play. But all that did was let them hoes tally up on the tab for the hotel, dinner, cab rides, etc. In their minds, I was blowing our money on these things for the benefit of a square bitch, while in my mind I was adding to my team.

I felt like a boss because I knew there was no way I'd ever do any of these things on just a booty call, so I assumed that my hoes knew this, and that should make all my moves stand up to any scrutiny. But the fact remained the same that I was doing too much for an unqualified bitch in the eyes of my folks, and I shouldn't have ever shared her existence with them until she was gettin' down with them. Period.

The thing about Separatism that makes it so very important is the way it closes the door to unnecessary bullshit that can interrupt the flow of your hustle. Yeah, it's cool to be able to tell a bitch that you're down with your hoes enough to be in the trenches with them, but the particular level of loneliness that comes along with being a real pimp pushed me to share more with my folks than they needed to know. I should've separated the pimp business from the hoes' business until it became ho business. That would've occurred when the square bitch became a prostitute. How else could I expect a ho to understand or respect it completely?

Until a ho was involved, it was not ho business. And if I wanted to keep it real, then my only obligation was to make sure ol' girl became a prostitute in the end.

What I did was answer to some hoes who didn't know any answers. So, when the question of why I was doing all that came up, they drew a blank. Being too honest only served to confuse the situation. At that point, I had pimp business mixed up with ho business. And the ho business was mixed up on square business. That turned into my business bein' a mess. And messy business has no place in a pimp's program.

When you muddy the waters in which you swim, you can't see where you're trying to go anymore. That's when you lose your way. Then the best you can do is tread water or float. But that gets you nowhere. And if it's real bad for you, it'll become impossible to tell which way is down and which way is up. In that kind of situation, your every move might be takin' you deeper into your mess until you're bound to drown.

That one bad situation, as any one bad situation can be, was the opening for all kinds of things to start going wrong in my mix. Because once bad habits begin, they can be hard or impossible to break.

Another example of going wrong by not applying Separatism can be found in how "friends" can bring you down in life. I remember a time when I was into the dope dealing thing and some of my gangster buddies robbed one of my baller buddies. The baller buddy was a guy I bought my packages from, so he was my plug. One of the guys on the block hooked me up with the dude and I made a lot of money fuckin' with him.

After a while, he opened up to me. He showed me his jewelry, had me meet him by one of his spots, and just trusted me more than others in general. But he made a move I didn't like. Once, after coppin' some work from him, he called me and told me my money was short.

My boys on the block were real gunslingers who had love for me. They saw this dude coming and going when he did business with me. And being my peoples, they knew more than they should about how much I was buying, so indirectly they peeped that dude's level was higher than they originally thought.

My boys left dude alone as long as he was cool with me, but I made a mistake. Actually, I made three or four mistakes. First, I mentioned the jewelry he'd shown me without thinking that, if he wanted people to know, he could've worn it when he came to the hood. Next, I complained to one of my boys about the short-change move the baller dude pulled on me when I was trying to figure out how the money ended up funny after I'd counted it twice before giving it to him. The real clincher was when I asked around to see if prices had gone up on coke in the hood because ol' boy started charging me more. Once I realized no one had raised their prices except for my plug, I was unhappy, of course. So once again I complained to my buddy from the block.

Little did I know, my boy was just waiting for me to stop fuckin' with ol' boy so he could go rob him. And as soon as he knew I bought a package from someone else, that's exactly what he did.

But ol' boy wasn't no punk. He came back that same day and shot one of my boys six times up close. Then he sent word through the guy on the block who hooked me up with him that he wanted his jewelry and money back or he was coming back to rock and roll again.

Lucky for me, my peoples was just as serious about shooting as he was, or I might be dead right now. Because in not knowing what had gone down, I called dude tryin' to cop some work. But he thought it was a set-up instead of an opportunity to smoke another member of my squad, so he avoided me instead of coming after me.

Sad part about it is he could've easily gotten me, too. Because my "friends" never told me what they were going to do, or that they'd done it, so I wasn't even thinking in terms of protecting myself from this dude. I could've and would've walked blindly into my own worst nightmare without even knowing it.

Around my way, when you speak to people on things that you may happen to have seen, or that you know about another person, they call it pillow talking. I was guilty of pillow talking in that situation. I was young, and it was stupid. I meant no harm at all, but my mistake led to robbery, shootings, and at least one murder.

If I would have known to keep my gangster buddies and my baller buddy separated on my playing field, none of this would have taken place. Furthermore, if I was out there about money, I should've separated myself from the gunslingers in my area.

It's OK to outgrow people in life when you know you're on the path you've chosen for yourself. Especially when your path is moving forward and those other people are doing the same kind of things you've decided to leave behind. Once I started submerging myself in the hustle of handling hoes, I had no choice other than to separate myself from all I've done before.

A lot of things must end at the point where pimpin' begins. If you want it to work, you must commit yourself to making sure it does. Part of that commitment is the act of separating yourself from whatever doesn't add to your pimpish pursuits in life.

Of course, you want to feel like you're keepin' it real with people you came up with or know from back in the day. That's what kept me in touch with my buddies from the block more than anything else. But real people do real things no matter what. So you don't have to hang around just to feel like you're keepin' it real. You can show your face or lend a helping hand whenever you want or need to. And all that can be done while still remaining separate in a way that you're not involved or affected by whatever is goin' on with those people in your life.

The Bible says, "Be in the world, but not of the world." I think Separatism is what was being talked about in that verse.

When whatever metal you're lookin' for comes out of the ground, it must first be separated from the dirt in which is was found. This goes for gold, silver, copper, lead, iron, or steel. If you want to be anything worth something, you must separate the things that are not in line with that thing you're supposed to be. It's a purifying process. You burn away the dross to raise the value of what is left behind. And there is nothing on earth that is pure without it first being kept or made to become separate.

All Ism is absolute, but this particular principle is at the top of the list as far as being non-negotiable. The Game we're in is far too delicate of a balance for anything to be in it that doesn't belong there. Any woman who is on your team must be purely all for you. And everything you do must remain purely away from all the things outside of what your hustle consists of.

Pimpin' must be pure...

So, Separatism is a must in all ways, at all times.

Now, if the whole idea behind the concept of Game is to know all the ways to work your play, then obviously we can look at this principle of Separatism in yet another way.

A lot of people in this world of hustle can honestly say that they never saw a real large-scale level of success until they hit the highway. There's something about gettin' it on the road that adds a seriousness to your approach. And with greater risk comes greater reward. So you will usually see a greater amount of money when you separate yourself and your team from the home base. This is because it increases focus and zooms the mind in on what you're there for. It's also because of the fact that you've done away with your safety net.

Being close to home is like having a parachute. Going to another town is like doing away with the parachute. That leaves you no choice other than to depend on your wings. This is when we discover who can fly.

When you separate your team from wherever you found them, they will depend more upon your instruction. Because the new place is unfamiliar territory, you become the only thing they know.

This can also bring your folks closer together, since they won't know any of the other hoes around them and will appreciate the need to have each other's back.

As long as your business is not a mess to begin with, this form of Separatism can only bring beneficial results to anyone who uses it in his program.

In my opinion, Separatism of this kind serves to purify your situation because it removes all distractions. There are no friends around to sidetrack anybody, no hangout spots off location to duck off into – things like that. A mistake in this Game can cost you a lot; maybe even your life. So the situation demands that you put your best foot forward with every step you take.

If your pimpin' is not real, you need to tighten it up. But if your pimpin' is real, it can only grow from learning how to separate your ho from the places she knows. And it's not just about putting her at a disadvantage, either. She will benefit just as much from the effect that separation has upon you.

Remember that you're a team. So most things that you come across in pursuit of your dream will work both ways. You'll depend on her as much as she depends on you. You'll need focus as much as she does. And if you don't have it, then you cannot expect her to.

I remember turning out a young cutie from San Francisco once. We dipped around the Bay Area for a few months at first and did OK. But greatness didn't come until I took her out the Los Angeles to get our money.

We went from getting three to five hundred a day to getting seven hundred to a thousand a day. All I had to do was wake her up and keep it pimpin'. She did the rest on her own.

One day I asked her what the difference was and she looked at me like I was stupid. Then she said, "Ain't shit else out here to do except what we came here to do." She didn't drink or smoke at the time, and being only 19 or 20 years old, she wasn't gettin' in any clubs. So from the time she woke up at checkout to pay the hotel until the sun came up the next day, all she wanted was to get paid.

There was another one I came across in the Midwest somewhere who was comfortable just kickin' it with me until I took her out to Chicago. Once we hit that Chi-Town area, her work ethic kicked into another gear. It was like the difference between night and day. But she was no longer surrounded by a bunch of friends who were all just laying around being lazy. So naturally the situation's isolation erased that social contamination, and without the contamination, ol' girl was a much better individual.

As fast as New York is, I've come across good hoes who had no clue how good they were until I got them down into Virginia with me. I've had hoes out of Boston and Philadelphia who barely even wanted to turn a trick until I got them into New Jersey where nobody knew them. So there's a lot to be said for the value of separating a new member of your team from the surroundings that you found her in.

Separatism is the formula-finding-part of your pimpin' that determines what you should be and should not be putting into your program. Because everything doesn't mix well, and certain things aren't even meant to be mixed with each other.

Anyone who doesn't know about finding the right formula better learn. Or that person is going to lose a lot more than they will earn, that's for sure. And just like with any other kind of chemistry, the wrong combination of ingredients can turn toxic, or even blow up in your face.

Find out what works well with your folks and separate them from all else. Once you do this, it is my advice that you do the same for yourself, as well. This includes both people and places. We even may as well throw in "things" while we're at it. Because as I write these words, my TV is off. If it was on, the quality of what you're reading would surely suffer.

And as for my own personal experience, I know that I do my biggest and best pimpin' when I'm by myself, so I don't bring my friends along for the ride. Even if they got hoes, too, I still find ways to maintain some sort of separation.

I remember before I developed this habit, I was so damn proud of how real my pimpin' was that I always welcomed an audience. But after a while, I noticed two things. The first thing was how my bankroll either grew very slowly or not at all whenever I hung out too much with my pimp buddies. This was because we was so busy "doin' it big" to prove to each other how "it's nothin" to a boss, we was spendin' our money as fast as we was makin' it. The other thing was how the people I hung with who wasn't pimpin' always needed help with something. And they knew I had money, so who do you think they came to for help?

And it's downright shameful to see how many hoes have mothers who will try and get on the gravy train if they are not the type to flip out once they learn their daughters are in the ho Game.

I had one little pimp buddy who told me about breakin' his ho once he saw she was tryna keep her money to herself. He let her get in the shower and emptied the bitch purse. What was so crazy about his story was that I expected him to tell me a trick called, or maybe some random dude. But he fucked me up when he told me it was the ho's mama who called him talkin' about how they really needed the bitch's ho money. That shit confused me so bad, I stopped talkin' to my young potna after he told me the story because I believe some things can be contagious, and I didn't wanna catch whatever had infected his program.

I had to separate myself from his association, because the principle of Separatism was a better friend to my pimpin' than ol' boy was, ya dig?

Separatism is where the control comes from in your Ism on a lot of different levels. This applies directly and indirectly towards both yourself and your team, as well as your overall situation as a whole, because you are cutting off negative influence and results when you put distance between your program and certain people, places, and things.

There are even times when I have to separate one part of myself from the other. That's literally the definition of having self-control. Because at the times when I failed to keep my pimp-related concerns above my normal human thoughts, my pimpin' usually suffered. Even in small ways, the overlooking of key considerations could lead to disaster. And there is no such thing as a "small" disaster.

Separatism ties in with Voyeurism (which we will discuss later) as related principles of Ism, because you must step away from the moment in order to not get caught up in it. That's the only way to watch everyone and everything enough to accurately see what you're looking at.

With the application of Voyeurism, you keep in mind to look both ways before crossing the street, as well as looking at the street itself. And with the application of Separatism, you enhance that practice with the measure of "stop, look, and listen" before you cross that same street. That extra measure can often be the difference between success and failure.

Think about it like this: If you're in a fishbowl, you can't see all directions at once. So in order to be able to see everything in all directions, you must be able to separate yourself from within the fishbowl.

From the outside looking in, you'll see the whole bowl at once instead of just the front, back, right, or left. So this particular aspect of Separatism – the personal aspect – holds any situation similar to the fishbowl. When socializing on your Ism, you must step out of the fishbowl by separating yourself enough to be aware. The awareness that your improved vision provides will keep your pimpin' free of doing what regular people do that can work against the success of your program.

For example, when that ho does something to hurt your little feelings, or make you mad, you gotta think. You don't have the luxury of freely expressing yourself. You have to really consider what the outcome of your reaction is going to be, and make an executive decision. And be enough of a boss to know when the Game is over, too. Because it might be time for the both of you to move on. The principle of Separatism would be incomplete if I didn't include this aspect of it, because everything is not meant to last forever. Even things that were once meant to be.

Seasons change, and so do people. Who you meet today may be a whole other person in a few years, or even a few months. There's no such thing as a pimp who kept every single ho he ever had. And the ones who tried to hold on to a bitch beyond her expiration date usually ended up on some page that had nothin' to do with pimpin'.

Be professional enough to remember that a lot of things in life come to an end at the point where pimpin' begins. This includes sentimental connections. Therefore, when a ho is no longer a ho, or she's no longer *your* ho... it's time to go.

In this Game you may have to mingle with the exact same people you want to avoid. Every ho you get won't be a match made in heaven.

If pimpin' is your bread and meat, then if you don't win, you won't eat. This fact may make it a must that you accept a ho's contribution under circumstances you'd normally not accept. She may be the kind of ho you don't like. Or maybe you got her in a way you're not proud of. Whatever the case may be, once the uncompromising nature of that need goes away, you should separate yourself from that ho. Because as a person, she deserves more than bad results and disappointment. And as a professional, you wouldn't be unhappy about something that worked well for you, so if it's not working well, it may not end well, either.

This is why the principle of Separatism dictates that you take control of how it ends. Trust me when I tell you that the jailhouse is just lying in wait for the people who don't follow this advice.

On at least two separate occasions, I have found myself in a position that called for such separation without me answering the call. And in both of those situations, the police were able to use the same individuals against me that I had neglected to separate myself from. And the bad part is that it had already crossed my mind to leave both the women in both these situations. But I was waiting for both individuals to fall off instead of taking control and actively separating myself from them. And in each instance, it worked against me. So please believe that it's just as important to say "goodbye" as it is to say "hello."

Separatism keeps the rest of your Ism safe. Don't think you can survive without it, or your business will surely be a mess. I can guarantee it.

There have been times when I didn't want to feel as if I did something wrong. And that was the case with both the individuals mentioned above. But what I should've done was set something to the side for them. That way, when I cut them off, I left them feeling satisfied.

Money is truly the root of all evil. And when you get a lot of it with someone, you will sometimes see another side of that person.

Keep your principle of Voyeurism in play at all times to help you spot this development. Because if it shows its ugly face in your program, you'd better employ your Separatism if you want to avoid a bad outcome.

I say this because there are those out there who don't want you to go on doing good without them. There are even some who don't want you to go on doing good with them. These are the types that will make a goal out of bringing you down. You'll mistake her for a stepping-stone, when she's really a landmine. They're not hard to spot if you know what you're looking for. But if you miss the warning signs, they will blow your pimp program to pieces every time.

Your radar should beep overtime when you hear one of these types tell you or someone else how they are the "strong, independent" type. Then, if you listen to them talk, you'll hear them always speak on how some guy did them wrong or tried to "use" them. If you listen closer, over time you'll catch them speak of how they weren't going for one thing or another – like they are just so super Game tight, they just can't be played. It should get extra spooky when you hear them talk about how they aren't going to, or how they didn't allow someone to, "get away" with this or that. By this point, you should be recognizing a problem.

Now here is where the details will show you what is real about these walking disasters.

They always claim to be "there" for everybody, but they're constantly complaining about it.

They're always the victim in some story about how somebody fucked them over somehow.

They're always crying about how they're doing everything on their own and no one is there to help them.

These people never have anything to show for any kind of real success in life. You'll either see cute, cheap things in abundance, or it'll just be downright raggedy behind the scenes. This is because the mindset it takes to destroy everything, they touch will not allow them to build for themselves. If they do work a square job, they'll have a long record of quitting or getting fired, and usually whatever job they do get will be some bullshit.

If they're a hustler, they'll usually be flashy with no stable living arrangement, but they'll constantly talk about how can't nobody "handle" them.

They'll usually come into a situation trying to represent themselves as being extremely beneficial, but they'll only be doing superficial things to draw you in. Every single square chick I ever met who fit this category followed this path by trying to feed me. They really believe that the key to a man's heart is through his stomach. And all the hustlers I came across who were this type would break you off in the beginning, but then say things that let you know they don't plan to break you off for long.

Every bit of this is just bait. If you bite, you will fall into a pit of deception. Disappointment, finger pointing, and ultimatums are what you will discover before long. You'll find yourself in arguments without knowing how you got there. The first chance she gets to react to anything you've done; the reaction will be super overboard. Or you'll find yourself talking her out of hating herself for some part of her past that she won't specify but knows she should be judged for.

The really bad cases are the ones who will talk about some part of their past that they know they should be judged for, but expect you to say it's cool. If you come across this kind, test her every time. Tell her the ugly truth about what she did. This doesn't mean you judge her for it. But if she can't admit to that ugly truth, then she doesn't think is was ugly, or she doesn't think that's what *you* should think.

In either case, you're dealing with a depraved mind that is not working with a conscience. If they don't feel bad for what they did, they won't feel bad for what they will do.

And that should be a major stop sign for you.

Separating from these types as soon and as smoothly as possible is what I suggest. And until you know a woman is not one of these types, you should not be letting her know too much of your business. She'll be exactly who makes that call to the cops with an anonymous tip about what you got in your house. She'll be the one calling your main bitch, or all of your bitches, with some scandal-causing conversation to create drama in your life. And it doesn't matter if you keep shit official, because she'll make things up in a heartbeat.

This is the bitch who will be talking to a head-busta about robbing you. I even had one clown telling random people where I lived and what I had. Her goal was to get my house broken into.

Pit bulls all over my yard on chains in strategic places kept me safe from this kind of occurrence. But recognizing a disaster ahead of time would've worked even better.

These kinds of individuals are more dangerous than anything else. Because everything else that can hurt you will usually be unable to find you until these types bring you to their attention.

So, when you're running through bitches, be sure to watch your steps closely enough to avoid these landmines. Because they're out there waiting to blow your program to pieces. And it's best to use this aspect of Separatism to remain separate from these types at all cost.

There are strong, independent women out there. Don't get it twisted. But I'm warning against these rotten apples who are actually weak and undependable. Those who are in reality depending on someone else's downfall or loss in order to feel some kind of victory in life. They are the misery-that-loves-company kind of Garbage Pail Kids I'm saying people should separate themselves from, because if they're not already doing it big for themselves, how will they ever do it big for you? That sounds like a one-way trip to Loserville if you ask me.

So, pull the plug on that mission as soon as you see you've stumbled up on one of these. You'll go further starting over than you will on that dead-end road for sure.

MYSTICISM

"Be like water, my friend."
– Bruce Lee

There are things in this world that happen or exist in a way that defies explanation. Over the course of history there are countless examples of this fact and how it affected the people involved with each episode.

Many times, a misperception was what the whole situation narrowed down to in the end. People either misunderstood what happened, or had no understanding at all about it. If there is a central figure or point of focus that these mysteries are attached to, then the mystery can often create a mythical quality or energy about that point of focus.

The nature of human beings is to either fear or worship what they don't fully understand, and there are those who will also just blindly hate it. It serves a pimp well to be aware of these facts, and consider them at all times, because some degree of mystery should always remain and even be cultivated carefully into your program as a part of your Ism.

This can be done easily by keeping the details of your business to yourself. Don't brag on how you make your play work. Just make it work and let others do the extra talking.

A lot gets twisted up in translation, because people think and speak in many different ways. So, when someone sees or hears something, it may come across to them differently than it does someone else. The reason for this can be as complicated as language barriers, or as simple as intelligence levels. A lack of intelligence doesn't mean stupidity any more than speaking a different language does. Let me explain.

Intelligence, when I use it in this particular segment of the script, means information. Nothing more, nothing less.

Now, I believe in God just like a lot of other people. I believe there was a Jesus, too. I even think that Jesus was a very special and important person who tried to lead a lot of people to God.

But I also believe that a very different language was spoken back when Jesus was alive. And the Bible was not first written in English, someone translated it. So through translation, we are now led to believe that Jesus did things normal people can't do. He had a mystical quality to him because we don't fully understand the way he connected with God.

I'm not trying to preach. My point it to show how powerful it is for people to not have all the details on how you do your thing. That's all. And that power is very valuable to any person in pursuit of a leadership position. It just so happens that pimps lead hoes. And if you're a good one, you'll lead them to where they want to be, yet never would've gotten to without you.

A magician never gives up his secrets. So when you see his show, you call what he does "magic," even though you yourself could learn to do the same things if only he would show you how.

That mystical quality the magician has is what you should possess to some degree. At least enough to keep your audience entertained and in recognition of your intelligence level being somewhat superior.

Loose lips sink ships. So even though you should have a lot to say, you should never reveal too much about yourself. Teach without revealing. . . Show without sharing.

The world and the universe are themselves miracles already. But your use of Separatism should keep you contained from showing the same surprise as your team whenever this fact reveals itself. This is one way that the general rule of acting cool will take you further than you think it can. Because if you show no surprise, then what do you know that everyone else doesn't? Maybe you even made it happen?

That's how Mysticism works. It may be seen by some as a strain on honesty at certain points, but your use of Socialism will keep you from any bad outcome as long as you care for the wants and needs of your team. Once you get them where they want to be, their gratuity should outweigh any guilt that can be placed upon you for any reason. The end result will justify the means.

I remember meeting one of the best hoes I ever had one day online. At the time she was out of reach, in another state, so we couldn't link up. But we got really tight on the phone for a few weeks before we faded away in each other's minds.

We talked a lot and shared personal details that you don't tell people every day. So, the seed was planted, but it would need time, patience, and a miracle to grow.

As I said before, miracles do exist in real life. And when one day the universe threw a miracle my way, I went right to work on it.

Years after I met that girl online, I saw her walking down the street in California, gettin' down as a prostitute. I remembered her face and most of what she told me about herself, but could not remember her name. So, I leaned heavy upon the power of my Ism and got real mystical on her when I finally got her to listen to what I was saying to her. When I was done runnin' my mouth, the picture that was painted was one of miracles and magic that left us no choice about what we should be doin' next.

I had that ho for three or four years after that. And it was through her that I discovered the value of Mysticism. Having enough experience by that time to know I should stick with what got the ball bouncin' in the first place, I just kept it mystical.

In the end, I didn't exercise enough Separatism with her, but before we reached that point of parting company, we got more together with each other than either one of us ever had before.

The whole situation was so unbelievable, I wrote a book about it – *A.O.B.* Just about every detail about that part of the story was the truth. But what no one would ever know is how important the principle of Mysticism was in making all that stuff happen.

In her eyes, I had a power that gave me a control over what was happening. This was because I treated everything that came our way in a certain fashion that gained her respect, while leaving some degree of mystery. Her faith in me having this power is what made this power come to life, because I was then responsible for making real results take shape for us.

I remember one time she caught a big-money trick in Las Vegas who fell in love with her. He would come every day to see her and pay her to hang out with him. So when she told me about him, I started coaching her on a million different lies to tell this dude. All the lies would boil down to reasons why she needed money, of course.

At first, I noticed that all he was to her was a legitimate excuse to take off from work and still get paid, so she didn't really want to burn him out or screw him over because he made her daily life that much easier. So, in order to pull her over to my way of thinking, I told her I was working on getting us a house. And because of this, we had to get some fast lumps and chunks of money, as any day the play might go down.

So, when she played her part, the ball was then in my court, forcing me to play my part. I didn't actually expect her to follow my instructions so well that we got exactly what I said we would. But when she did, I made sure I found a way to deliver on my promises.

That's the key to Mysticism. You don't just spin a web to have a ho caught up for no reason. You walk her through the process of making things actually happen. But you do it in a way that amazes her with how you did it. You want her to believe that no one else could have done it the way you did it.

Many of the other Ism principles tie in with the principle of Mysticism because you don't explain the details of what you do. And when your outcome looks amazing, you leave it at that. Let it define you.

It's not an act. It's not a scam. So don't see it or treat it like one. It's just another level to your Ism that will give your team the confidence they deserve. It's something more to believe in, that everybody should be able to have in life. And the principle of Realism dictates that you turn the dreams you sell into reality.

I suggest trying to always be conscious of opportunity to exploit mystical circumstances. They happen a lot more than people think. And it doesn't take any grand gesture to point out these things as they occur. All you have to do is pay attention and stretch the meaning of each one as far as you can, then keep it pushin'. The rest of the magic will happen somewhere in between the universe and the mind of your audience.

I've noticed that as my experience grows, I can almost predict certain things about hoes. After seeing something happen so many times, it becomes as easy as two plus two making four. But when I surprise a bitch by telling her about herself, I don't explain all this to her. I just leave it at the fact that I know. And since she can't explain how I know, it becomes "unexplainable" and "magical." Now, I'm either damn near psychic, or I'm so "in tune" with her that she just "knows" we were meant to be. Because as far as she's concerned, something kind of mystical happened. And I'm inclined to leave it at that.

One time, one of my providers busted a fucked up move and was somehow dumb enough to accidently catch herself on the video feature of her cell phone. So, on a routine check, I came across this piece of video she didn't even know she possessed. (It was so incomplete; I know it was unintentionally taken as she put the phone in her pocket.)

What I did was put that in my memory bank and kept it pimpin' until I got a good chance to throw it into the mix. But I wasn't interested in lies or excuses, so I didn't speak on it in the form of a question or accusation. And I "never" go through phones, so why would I admit to doing it now?

What I did instead was led her into saying some self-serving statement. Then I agreed with her and praised her for not being the type of ho who would do exactly what I knew she had done. And, of course, she knew she did it, but would never admit it if she didn't think she had to. So, she took the props I gave her, knowing good and well she didn't deserve them.

Sometimes you catch a sucker by playing like you're a sucker yourself. So, I pimped past her denial by delivering my message as if I was unaware of what I was doing. Then I dropped a couple of details to make sure she had to really wonder. After that I dropped some lugs on her about how impossible it is to dodge the Game when the Game is real. By the time I was done, ol' girl didn't know if it was God or the goddamn Devil talking through me. But I saw the goosebumps pop up on her arms and legs. And I got more out of that one ho than I have out of two or three bitches at once who were all badder bitches than she was. Because after that, my mind was to be respected right along with everything else that came out of my mouth.

I got mystical on that bitch...

And that's just one example. But if you apply the bonus lesson of Game itself, you'll remember that there are as many versions of that same play as there are the number of situations that life deals out to you. Just like the cards in a deck....

Mysticism is the part of your Ism that will lead into the flamboyant presentation pimps are known for. Because all of that is what will cast a spell on those who come under your influence.

In that way I'd have to say that this is the reinforcing principle to Hypnotism, because it is the presentation of what sets you apart in people's mind. And it also locks into place how and why you're so special.

The key is to put your twist on it as an individual. That way it's unique. This is where the bright colors and the animal skin interior on cars comes into play. It's the idea behind the gold rims and diamonds in people's teeth.

In ancient Aztec, Mayan, and Egyptian cultures, big jewelry was worn to show that a person was next to God. In Egypt it meant he was God. And in more recent times, like the royalty era in Europe or Asia, it was worn by Kings and

Queens. So that should tell you all you need to know about the effect that big jewelry can have upon those who see it, as well as the power it can give to those who wear it.

The same goes for beautiful clothes that come in every color of the rainbow. There's something special about making sure you're noticeable in something real exclusive when you come through. You need look no further than the animal kingdom for proof of this fact. The lion has a big bushy mane. A lot of birds have bright colorful feathers. All species of grass eaters, from deer to cattle to goats, have horns and antlers on their heads.

Nature dictates that the male of the species be very decorated. And among humans, he who can decorate his woman most is usually recognized as successful.

So, on a level of natural instinct, it's a pimp's professional priority to be over the top with how he dresses himself, what kinds of car he drives, and what kind of home he has. Whether it be in the brand name quality, the quantity of how much he has, or the noticeable colors he chooses.

Personally, I'm not into a lot of bright colors. But I make up for that with the brand name quality of what I buy myself. I've knocked more than a few females just on the strength of the fact that every time they saw me, I had on a different pair of some exclusive shoes. One chick told me that there was just something special about the fact that my feet never got dirty. And she couldn't stop herself from being attracted to that.

I knocked my first baby mama by standing in a crowd of niggas who were wearing white Ts and expensive shoes, while I wore Gucci from my head to my feet.

Whenever I've heard about people speaking of those out-of-body experiences, they all seem so drawn to the white light. It's like in a sea of darkness, that white light is seriously soothing to their soul. It calls to them and they're drawn to it.

Well, whenever a woman takes in the scenery around me. . . that white light is what I'm trying to be!

I remember I had a Mazda minivan I used to mob around in because it was low profile (and good on gas). But at the same time, I had a '94 Impala Super Sport fresh out the paint shop, on rims, with hella beat in it. Being in Stockton, California at the time, I usually kept a pistol on me. So it was safer to ride around in the minivan than take a chance on getting pulled over in the flashy Impala.

Now, I got a pretty good mouthpiece on me, so I could pull bitches in my minivan as easy as I could in my Super Sport. But of course, one would think that the big bubble Chevy on rims got me more bitches in the end, right? However, this was not the case – even though that Chevy got me noticed, and it did get me a lot of pussy. But I'm talkin' about really pullin' bitches into wanting to get with my program. Like, attach their life to my life type of shit.

The ones who fell into that more worthwhile category were almost exclusively made up of those who saw me in both vehicles, not just the fixed-up flashy one. This is because the average dude with a clean-ass car won't be driving around in a bucket. And the average dude driving a bucket can't afford a clean-ass car. But I would hop out the minivan dressed fresh to death with diamond pieces around my neck and fly kicks on my feet, so I obviously wasn't broke. And I know that it's a sucka move to go around tellin' everyone that you got a blower on you, so I wasn't lettin' it be known that I was strapped. Therefore, it remained a mystery why I wasn't always coming through on either one level or the other. And my ability to bounce back and forth between the two so inexplicably gave me a quality that caused the curiosity to reel 'em in.

The unexplainable became mystical...

There was another time when I was in Iowa trying to turn out a thick lil cornfed snowbunny. She liked me but she wasn't sure she wanted to be a ho. I think she was made of the right stuff, but she had a hard time knowing who she could trust.

When I peeped that last part, I played patient, because at least she wasn't sayin' no, and I was very far from home in serious need of a ho.

I could've tricked her into it, but she was so hung up on trust issues that my Voyeurism let me see that she'd be gone if she ever caught wind of what I had done. And no matter how desperate I become, I refuse to force anyone to ever do anything for me, because at all times, I take pride in my craftsmanship. So here's how I used the principle of Mysticism to win in that situation.

The first thing I did was let her get an eyeful of the fact that I was only working with a few hundred dollars. This was easy because I knew her paranoia would make her nosy. So all I had to do was send her to use my debit card in a way that would get the receipt with my balance on it.

Then, I got to bragging about how I was a real money man, but I was sure to put so many extras on it, I knew she would wonder why I didn't even have a thousand dollars to my name. What she didn't know was that I'd just left a ho who wanted to argue more than she wanted to get money, and that there is no way I would have done that without making sure I'd be straight. All I was waiting for was taxes to come through, and my sugar mama back in Las Vegas was going to send me a few stacks. This would be happening any day now, and it was the only reason why I was being patient with the chick in Iowa – because it gave me time to wait on that money without paying for a motel every day.

I knew the balance on my debit card would be bumped up soon. So, in order to take her mind elsewhere, I started ask about the weed prices out there, and she called around to find out what the ticket on a pound of the good-good was.

When she told me a number close to four thousand dollars, I called a little boyish bitch over from across the street, then I double-checked the info ol' girl gave me right in her face. But the real reason I did this was so that I could talk numbers in front of her.

Remember, she was paranoid about gettin' played, so she would surely question anything I said to her directly, but she would believe what she told herself. And with that in mind, I just put things in front of her to see and hear. Just a little bit of long-range Hypnotism.

The thing is, I had to walk her through the process of hypnotizing herself. So, I had to plant my suggestions creatively in order for her to discover them and then suggest them to herself.

But my Realism made this possible. Because I'm a real Bay boy. That means I come from where the best weed in the world first found its street value. And we been runnin' that shit up and down the highway like it was coke for the longest.

With that being said, I got hella potnas that are ballin' off the weed hustle, so of course I called one of my folks on the phone and ordered up a couple of Ps to be sent in the mail.

When the Teddy Bear showed up stuffed with a couple of elbows, I didn't make no noise about it. I was still waiting for the tax money to hit. I wasn't waiting long, though, because a couple days later, I got a text from the chick in Las

Vegas. And since I was on stage, I had her call me so I could put her on loudspeaker in front of ol' girl.

"Hey, Manny! I'm just trying to see if three thousand is enough?" my sugar mama said as soon as I connected the call.

Of course, this raised the antenna on ol' girl's ear-hustlin' surveillance system.

"Yeah, that'll work; if it's what you wanna send. As long as you know you don't gotta send me nothin' if you don't want to," I said back, just so she'd beg me to take the money.

"No, no! I want you to have it and do your thing with it. I know you could turn it into more, so I'm gonna send it. Just give me your debit card info and I'll do the transfer right now."

We made the move and ol' girl was a witness. Her mental conclusion was like a cake I had baked, and the cherry on top was when I ripped the Teddy Bear open to show her the trees I had as well.

"So, somebody just sent you three grand on your debit card, and you got over seven grand in weed? All that in less than a week? That's over ten grand that people just handed over, just like that?" she said as her mind did the math.

She didn't know if the weed was paid for or not. And I didn't tell her. She didn't know that ol' girl who sent me that money thought I was gonna double it up and give it back. And I didn't tell her that, either.

What she did know is that people who knew me a lot better than she did knew it was OK to put a lot in my hands. And I made sure I told her that, because she would tell herself that she saw this with her own eyes. And even though she had no explanation about why, the proof was the truth.

My Realism paved the way for a mystical example that was undeniable...

The next week we were in Chicago, and she was a full-time prostitute. Her friends were hating on her decisions, but she was confident in it because she'd seen for herself that somehow, someway, I was a man who could make things happen bigger and better than anything any of them had ever shown her in bum-fuck Iowa.

And that was enough to let her know that I had no need to play her. That I was worthy of her investment. And if she didn't jump on this opportunity, some other girl would, because other people were already in the mix and benefitting from taking chances on me.

In actuality, I never played this individual. What I did was play my hand in a way that put a spin on my Realism. That way, I could show who I was and how I got down in a way ol' girl wasn't used to seeing.

The mystical effect came from how her world was so unaccustomed to what she saw me being able to do. And all I did was let her see my personal business while not explaining the details to her.

That's the art of applying Mysticism. You keep it real without simplifying your reality with too much explanation. Then you allow for a little bit of sauce in the pursuit of showmanship on your part. And when you see that they're thinking, "Wow! How did that happen?" that's right where you let it remain.

It's reality, based on impressive points of your Realism, real artistic in its delivery. That artistic delivery is the sauce. Jewelry and dope rides are also the sauce. So are nice clothes and expensive shoes. These are all sauce. And having all your extras in place is what will make you saucy as a pimp. Mac Dre said he stayed "dipped in sauce." This is what he meant by that.

You should be so saucy that you sling and drip that sauce onto everything that you do. And that enhanced flavor is the resulting Mysticism of your reality, because things won't taste the same as they do when you serve it up. That's what makes you mystical, because certain things are only there because of you. And this is what makes you more than anything else they've seen or had before. This is how you manufacture your Mack Magic and your Mack Miracles.

The Me-Too movement would say I'm telling you how to manipulate a woman. But manipulation is when you influence someone in order to deceive them. Now, some may read these words and come up with ways to deceive women. But that's the same thing a whole shit load of preachers have been doing with the Bible for years. Doesn't make the Bible a bad book, though, so don't put that evil on me.

These words are written with attraction, enticement, and the gaining of mutual understandings in mind. Not deception.

One of the principles would not be Realism if I was trying to show you guys how to fake a woman out. So, if someone called this a manipulation manual, it would be them who's trying to do the manipulating. That's the thing about people who point fingers: they never look at their hand close enough to see that three fingers are pointing right back at them...

Mysticism is no different from the colorful package or the noticeable sign at your favorite store. It's your personal flair that distinguishes your brand. That's all. It's the "secret" part of your secret sauce. It's what keeps your customers coming back. It's what makes them happy they came to your establishment rather than someone else's.

Mysticism is the advertisement, quality control, and customer service all at the same time. And a productive marketing strategy is never a bad thing. No business can prosper without one in place, no matter how good the product might be.

In the Native American tribal history, they always had a medicine man who had so much influence, he may as well be the chief of the tribe. He had all the Game on herbal concoctions to fix whatever may be going wrong with a member of the tribe. And even if someone else went and picked the exact same herbs, they couldn't replace the medicine man, because only the medicine man knew what to do with those herbs.

A woman in the tribe wasn't a woman until the medicine man declared she was a woman.

A warrior was nobody until the medicine mad told the chief what kind of mission to send that fool on to prove himself. Even the chief wasn't official until ol' Mr. Medicine Manny Man let the tribe know that dude was the chosen one.

The medicine man didn't have to hunt; his cut came off the top. He didn't have to live in the community; he had his own spot off to the side that was usually private and bigger, because he was important and had more tools, so he needed more room or space than everybody else.

He could read minds at times, and nobody knew exactly how old he was. He didn't dress like the rest of the tribe, and either he was above needing any pussy, or he broke all the virgins in before they were open to the public – whatever he thought was best.

He had all the weed, because he had the peace pipe. He made all the pruno, so he decided when everybody could drink.

But he let the chief be the man most of the time and played the background, because the chief might change, but the medicine man remained the same.

The medicine man had that mystical aura about himself, and he used his Mysticism to maximum effect. He only gave the Game to someone else when it was his time to die. And until then, he was the boss behind the boss. He was the wise man of the group.

That's what Mysticism does to a pimp's program. It sets him apart and above the rest of mankind. It gives you your own palace in a ho's memory. It creates the cloud of respect that should surround you wherever you go.

Mastering this principle is what will make you legendary. It'll keep you spoken of highly, because your audience will be in awe of you.

So collect your ingredients, make your own secret sauce, and use that recipe for everything you do. Then dip yourself in that sauce every day. That way, you get it all over the place. And you'll see that the Game will bring you whatever you're trying to attract to yourself, because the only way they can experience that flavor is with you.

Mysticism makes the difference between a square and a pimp. And the level one possesses is what specifies the way that some pimps are just pimps, and others become Macks.

ACTIVISM

"Talk is cheap."
– Old Street Saying

So, one thing for sure in the street life is that, if you're all talk and no action, you're a joke. Period. You have to be about that action if you hope to ever get anywhere with anything in this life. This is where the principle of Activism comes into play.

Are you on stage, or in the audience? I could tell all this information to a parrot and he could repeat it word for word, but his brain will still only be about as big as a walnut. So surely, we must see how bird-brained it would be to settle for just talking about Game. Who you are is defined by how you act on what you know.

In the Bay, it was always easy to get a chance to make your mark, because Game was everywhere, all the time. But everybody didn't do the right things with their chances, so they never got a shot. Your chance was the opportunity to be somebody. So, it was nothin' special for a person's conversation or associations to place him is the presence of some very real aspect of this Game.

But when that prostitute was in your face asking you what's up, or your potnas handed you that military-grade weapon, or the biggest baller in your hood pulled you over and offered you that deal of a lifetime – you better make the right move. Because saying the right thing won't do you any good beyond that point.

It's about that action...

So when the O.G. pimps would pull up with bitches in their car who I knew from high school, I didn't just whisper about it to my niggas. They was doin' enough of that amongst themselves, because we all knew her. What I wanted was pimpin' to she that she would talk to me, so I spoke to the ho. I wasn't satisfied to just say I knew her, I had to *show* that I knew her. And the other youngstas wasn't doin' this.

Back when everybody was sellin' rocks on the block, I was one of the main ones tryna re-up all the time. It wasn't enough to say I knew the man. I had to *show* that I knew the man.

So when those real factors would hit the block in their clean-ass cars, I was flaggin' them down to double up whatever money I had, whether I needed to or not, just so I could take that ride around the block.

After a while, the pimps and ballers knew my face more and more from standing out around town. And most of the regular heads from block to block knew my face in connection with the more respected individuals. This made people identify me with more respected activity. And believe it or not, this has saved my life a lot more than my pistol ever did.

I remember back in the beginning of my journey, I had a potna named Darryl Mason from North Richmond. Everybody knew Darryl everywhere we went, so through him, I got comfortable in some real dangerous spots. But lucky for me, I've always been the type to want to stand on my own, because only depending on being able to say I knew Darryl might've cost me my life.

How it happened was that, outside of North Richmond, I used to see this dude named Troy around town in his old-school Monte Carlo, fuckin' with bitches and smokin' weed. I recognized his face from around Darryl's house in North Richmond, so whenever we came across each other in traffic, I would say what's up, and go out of my way to acknowledge him. Nothin' real major – just speakin' instead of peakin'.

Now, at the time, North Richmond was on a real serious war path. So what I was doing was a lot different than what the average dude would do when he ran into someone from that side of town. See, it wasn't enough for me to be able to say I be in North Richmond sometimes, I had to act on it when I saw a familiar face. And even though I'm not from North Richmond myself, I felt like I was cool with some real-ass niggas when I got down on that side of town.

One day, walking from Darryl's house on Sanford, I bumped into a lil nigga who was probably just as ambitious as I was, and he didn't know my face. The problem with that was the fact that we were in North Richmond, and *he* was *from* North Richmond. To make matters worse, I had left Darryl at his house, and I had a square-ass nigga with me who wasn't from the South Side, but he lived on the South Side. And the more I think about it, the more I'm sure it was his fault this lil nigga was hittin' me up.

"S'up wit' it, bruh? Where the fuck you niggas from? What the fuck y'all doin' out here?" ol' boy said real nasty and aggressive as we walked past where he was posted on the block.

As soon as he said "Where the fuck y'all from?," I knew we was about to have a serious problem. And not really sure what I should say, I tried to just get away with, "S'up," while I kept it movin'.

But we was on our way back to the central side of town, which meant one of two things: One, we would be waiting on a bus that came to a bus stop two blocks away; or two, we would have to walk all the way out of North Richmond. And I could tell we was not about to make it far enough to choose either one of those options.

I couldn't get away with beatin' this lil dude up in his own hood. And he was definitely about to start some shit. And this was before cell phones were in everybody's life, so I couldn't just call Darryl. And as soon as it came out that the dude with me was from the South Side, we was about to get cooked!

So I dipped into the liquor store on the corner, hoping that the situation would go away. Maybe lil dude would just go on about his business, or somethin'.

I took my time in that corner store buying soda, chips, and a tamale out of the crock pot by the register up front. The whole time, I'm wondering how to make sure ol' boy was gone before I dipped out of the store. Then I decided to just go back to Darryl's house, instead of trying to escape. Maybe if I made it there, I could get a one-on-one with this dude.

However, as I'm paying for my shit at the register, in walks the same dude. And now he got the boys in black with him. Black hoodies, burner gloves, black sweats and shoes. . . with big bulges under their hoodies that only extended clips could make.

Bald heads and bad vibes blocked my way out of the store. Shit had shifted from serious to deadly, just that fast.

"Where you niggas from?" asked the biggest one in the bunch. But before I could say anything, the boy Troy walked into that store and saved my life.

"Man-Man, s'up wit' it?" he said out of reflex.

"S'up, Troy?" I said back.

That's when Troy took in the whole scene and saw what was about to go down. Thank God he knew every nigga in that hit squad. When he was done explaining who I was, the boys in black said, "Go on and get up outta here, Man-Man. You cool. Just come through by yourself from now on," and the whole issue along with the hit squad and the lil shit starter disappeared.

Every time I saw Troy after that, we would just laugh and he would only say, "Uh-huh." But that's when I knew that real things are what real niggas do. And if I wasn't real enough to act on the fact that I'd seen that man before at the times that I saw him, I would not be writing these words right now...

My employment of Activism is why I was able to come into prison already established as real, even though I'd not been there before. Hitters and head-bustas knew me from really bein' in it. At times and in places that no regular person would've ever dared to be, they remembered seein' me. My ghetto report card was A++, and the stamp on me was official. I was never no snitch or no bitch, and before I would ever have to bow down to someone, someone else would speak favorably on my name. So it wasn't no tough-guy shit that saved me. Even though shutting down the block a few times along the way didn't hurt, it was the fact that I did what any real individual would do that gave me that high score.

Being in real places around other real individuals worked in my favor. And doing real things, even if they wasn't big things, made me official.

There was a time when my track record even benefitted from gettin' the shit beat out of me. I had a potna from Fifteenth Street named Corey who lived deep on the south side of Richmond, on Potrero, between Kennedy Manor and Cresent Park. I was on the run for jumping bail on assault weapon charges in Santa Rosa, so I hid out at Corey's house and we just sold a little weed and stayed out of the way.

One night, though, Corey convinced me to go out with him and his girlfriend. They had popped some pills and would not accept that I wanted to stay at the house. The girlfriend even sweetened the deal by calling a bunch of her friends to come with us. So now I had my choice of about eight different women, and with that many heads, I knew I'd sell some weed, too. So I went along.

We ended up at the Berkeley Marina, ducked off from where everyone else was parked to look at the lights of San Francisco. Our little party was poppin' behind a row of trees that surrounded the parking lot to a restaurant that was closed for the night. Most of the people had popped a pill, and everybody was drinking, so you know the group was feelin' themselves. And it was cool because it was just us.

Until it wasn't just us anymore...

Everybody in the Bay knows about hangin' out at the Marina. From San Leandro all the way to Vallejo, the Marina is the spot when you're out and about with nowhere to go. And the one in Berkeley is the most popular.

For the most part, it's neutral territory, so you might run into someone from anywhere in the Bay at the Marina. But there's no place in the Bay that anyone should ever get caught slippin'; and I must admit, I was slippin' with my potna that night. We were two skinny niggas in a truck on rims with eight or nine bitches from Richmond. One of the females was in a candy-painted Camaro on rims, and both vehicles had beat in them with the music up loud. Plus, everybody was tipsy, so we was all talkin' shit. It was a recipe for disaster, because those females was gonna surely draw some nigga's attention, and that's exactly what happened.

First it was only one dude. Then it was two or three dudes. And they must have went and got they crew, because the next thing I knew, it was like a mini sideshow back there with us.

Two or three cars joined us in our secluded spot, and muthafuckas started doin' what we do in the Bay: Tyrna get noticed by the females. But every one of these new dudes was part of the same group. That's what made it ugly.

I hopped out the truck to get up on a female I was gettin' at. It was cool, but my buddy was with his girl, so he stayed in the truck. The problem was that all of these girls were her friends, so she was movin' back and forth between the truck and the crowd. And she had an ass like a whale tail, so pretty soon one of these other dudes got at her. I saw it, but I didn't trip too much because these dudes didn't seem like they was on no bullshit; just havin' fun in a mixed group and happened to come across some random chicks in traffic.

But then, one of them tried to get at my potna's girl, and kept at it even after she shined him on. Then my boy leaned out of the truck to let his presence be known. They exchanged a few words and the party went on, but now this dude is staying around the truck. Before long, he cracks at my boy's girl again, and that's where it all went bad.

My nigga Corey was totally stuntin' on a pill and drunk as a skunk, so as soon as words started exchanging, he took it there with this dude. I'm thinking he must have been strapped, or something, because there was no way was was gonna whoop all these fools. They was just as deep as the bitches we was with, if not deeper! But when ol' boy barked back and shit got tense, what did Corey do? He jumped his lil one-hundred-sixty-pound ass out of the damn truck like he was ten people!

So we mix it up with these dudes, and just as I expected, we got whooped. I mean, I can fight as long as I'm against one person. If things go my way, I might even handle two. But beyond that, it's cookies!

However, by the next day, all them females we was with was tellin' stories about how me and Corey was like Superman and fought a whole parking lot full of muthafuckas! And all the young hitters in that hood came through to check on us. We couldn't call no shot, because we never knew where these dudes was from, so they got away with it. But since then, I have never come across a youngsta from that little corner of Richmond who didn't treat me like he'd known me his whole life.   .

I never said I'm some kind of Superman, and you'll never hear me say I'm "the man"; even though, there may be stories out there about me that fit the description of both those terms. All I can say for sure is that I was a man, no matter where I may happen to stand. And whenever I have a choice, I try to leave people thinking good things about what kind of man I am.

Over the years, my name has come up in a few of murders. This is the case for most of the men who come from where I'm from. In one case, I said I seen the whole thing. Then I proceeded to tell an imaginary story about some completely non-existent dudes who did it. That brought my friend home after shooting a muthafucka in the head in front of the whole block. Nobody else talked, so my word set him free. He's no longer with us, so I can speak on this since I had nothing to do with his actions, of course.

In another case, I said a little too much about what I did. This was because I had two childhood friends with me and didn't want my actions to land them in prison. So I did my own time and rode my own case. They both went free, and I got manslaughter.

And on the other one, when my peoples did what they had it in 'em to do, it was done after it was done. So when the po-po grabbed me and asked me about it, there was never anything to say. Period.

I knew nothing, I saw nothing, I heard nothing, and I said nothing.

Imagine that...

In case the overall application of the Activism principle is still not completely clear, let me share some more examples with you.

This memory is about a widely-known pimp who may not want his business out there, so I'll just call him "Mr. Mack."

Mr. Mack had a big black 'Benz back in the day on gold rims. He was known far and wide for pimpin' on a ho, and people respect him till this very day. But there was one day when he pulled up to a place, and for some reason, another dude ended up spittin' on Mr. Mack's 'Benz. Well, Mr. Mack shot that dude for that. I never knew what the issue was, because the dude who got shot ended up being cool with me after I lived in his hood for a little while and started seem' him around. But he never told on Mr. Mack, and nobody ever spit on Mr. Mack's car again, either. They both acted in the way they were supposed to in that instance.

There's a certified ganster from Oakland who is pretty much on the level of Mob boss, who played in the pimp Game at one time. Most people on the track left his hoes alone, because nobody wanted to go through the fighting and shooting that ol' boy was notorious for. But Mr. Mack was in his business on them hoes, though. And when ol' boy did what he was known to do, he realized Mr. Mack wasn't a pushover. Shoot-outs are what came about when these two bumped heads.

There was another situation in which Mr. Mack and another Rich-Town pimp got jumped in San Francisco, on the track. They ended up in the hospital, fucked up and arguing about who did what while it was going down. But one thing for sure, though; neither of them ran away.

It may or may not be surprising to hear what I'm about to say next, especially to someone from someone other than where I'm from. But the God's honest truth is that, I got more pimp principles from two of the most serious gangsters I met in prison than anywhere else.

C-Moe from the South Side and Lil Nation from North Richmond are who I'm referring to with that statement. I met a lot of serious gangsters in prison, don't get it twisted. But these were two of them that gave me some tools I've used in my pimpin' pursuits.

C-Moe taught me so much that I'm convinced he shoud've been a pimp. But in the Bay Area, even a lot of white-collar criminals can get savage wit' it, so I can't say that if he was free when I met him that he wouldn't have been pimpin'.

He was almost fifteen years older than me, so maybe it was just his age group that gave him so much Game. All I know for sure is that, we used to chop it up a lot, about every subject of the Game. There was no question that I ever asked that C-Moe didn't know the answer to. And I'm grateful to have known him. He was sometime so goofy and playful, you'd think he was a real comedian. But if the wrong thing happened, he could cut that funny shit off like a light switch.

There was a time when we were hanging out with three other guys who were all members of the same organization. We were on a level 4 yard, so just about everybody had life sentences. This means it was a pretty safe bet to say that everybody you met had at least a 90 percent chance of being a killer.

So when a joke slipped into a comment C-Moe felt was disrespectful, things got real scary when he flipped that switch. That's when I saw with my own eyes a big-dog version of the puppy that I was. I won't get specific about what C-Moe did, because that's not my story to tell. But what I will say is that he did it so immediately, none of those dudes had a chance to prepare a defense. And I stood by his side from start to finish...

Special shout-out goes to the truth!

Lil Nation was more military with what he taught me, but his influences were clearly colored by pimpish principles. He would always tell me how he knew he should've been a pimp, but he also knew he'd fuck around and smoke somebody for playin'.

This was the first person who explained to me the principle of Hypnotism. But what he never knew was that, up until he mentioned it, I thought I was the only person who thought in this way. Lil Nation knew how powerful and important matters of the mind could be. And having control over self and others was a large part of the lessons he taught me. But as smart and slick as he was, there was always a dangerously rough element to how he approached anything he did.

I once saw Lil Nation "accidently" break a man's leg while playing baseball. He was supposed to be sliding into home base, but the move "somehow" turned into something like a football tackle. In the end, I always had to wonder if Nation was even going for the home plate at all.

The most memorable lesson I learned from him, however, was learned from the sideline. We were having a little Rich-Town picnic with burritos and shit. The whole car was there and the talk went into old stories. One of the subjects was who was new to this shit and who was true to this shit. Lil Nation had big money and a high hit score on the streets, and he was never shy about exercising his hard-earned braggin' rights.

But then another homeboy from his same age group decided to try and steal the spotlight with what he thought were some relevant facts.

"Yeah, you niggas was on it once y'all finally got in it. But I was gettin' money before anybody in our generation, though," the homie said with confidence.

But Lil Nation wasn't ruffled at all. He just asked politely, "Is you sayin' you got more money than me?"

"Naw, man, I won't lie. . . y'all niggas was gettin' it. But I been gettin' that shit since waaay back, though," the homie replied.

"Oh, well, last time I checked, it ain't how long you been in it, it's how strong you been in it," Lil Nation said, checkmating ol' boy.

And just that quick, that conversation was done. What else was there to say?

All I can tell you now is that, to this day, that is one of the realest things I've ever heard. And I've repeated it many times myself every since hearing it from Lil Nation.

Many years later, my peoples Lil Johnny called me from San Quentin and put Lil Nation on the phone. Once he remembered who I was, he asked what I was up to. I was somewhere on the east coast runnin' some hoes and told him so. His gold-trimmed smile came to mind as he laughed into the phone and said, "I always saw it in you, my nigga..."

And unless he happens to read these words, he may not ever know how much knowing him did for my Ism. Even that little exchange on the phone kicked my already-advanced pimpin' into another gear. I went on and bought myself some gold spoke rims just to remember how those niggas used to do it. And I swear, as funny as this may sound, I had my hoes doin' burpies every day after that for a few months.

I still got those old Daytons put up right now, just waitin' for the right old-school to come my way so I can slap some vouge tires on 'em and shit on some niggas. Because that, too, would be an employment of the Activism principle. Stickin' to the way niggas used to do it back in the day.

In case you haven't figured it out yet, the principle of Activism is simple: Stick to the G-Code. Don't be no bitch, don't be no snitch, fuck with real individuals, and don't just be talkin' about what you do, walk that shit out at all costs.

Activism is the other part – the co-part – of Realism. And there would be no Ism as all without it. Because either you'll never make it off the starting line, or somebody is gonna smack you as soon as you do.

The G-Code applies to anything you do in this Game at all. Pimp shit included, of course. But even if you was to square up and turn your life around, you should still apply it to the moves you make. Because in my humble opinion, the term G-Code doesn't mean "Gangster" Code. I think the "G" stands for "Genuine," which means real and authentic.

Don't ever let anything come along in life that makes you break the rule of sticking to this principle, because in all my years, it's kept me safer than any weapon. It's taught me more than any classroom, and it's paid my way when money wasn't on the menu. You want to keep it in one piece, unharmed, and intact. Because if it's not in working condition, you're in a bad position.

Even knowing the right move to make won't do you any good if you don't act on it. So get your Activism in order, stand tall through it all, and keep it real in the end. Stick to the G-Code! And never hesitate to get active about what a real individual is supposed to do. That's what will make you an activist who never fails to employ the principle of Activism...

Let me leave this subject with a piece of proof about just how important it is to be actively involved with doing real things.

I once had a friend who was a really good dude until he started playin' with his nose. I don't know if it was because he got on the blow so late in the Game, or if the blow just brought out something that he would normally know was best to keep hidden.

Whatever the case was, he went from one extreme to the next when it came to being believable, so after driving into San Francisco all the way from Arizona to fuck with him, I kind of fell out with him. After that, I faded off from fuckin' wit' dude, but while I went on about my business, my old buddy was stuck at his girl's house, mad at me. So while I went on my merry way into traffic, he was on some other shit.

Anyway, one day I came across a few people that I met through my old buddy, in Oakland. And just because I fell off with ol' boy, I saw no reason to stop fuckin' with the people he introduced me to.

There are two groups of people I'm referring to at this point. One was some cool cats out of Louisiana who owned a tire shop on East 14th, and the other was a couple of cats from High Street.

I got to fuckin' with the dudes from High Street real tough for a little while, and since one of them had the weed,

I used to take them up to the tire shop whenever those dudes called me about some trees. So basically, I was in the mix with both groups of people on an almost daily basis, and over the course of these months, my old buddy wasn't even comin' outside.

Then, one day, I'm in the house off High Street gettin' dusty with these dudes, and my old buddy calls one of them on the phone. By then, we all knew this man was goin' crazy off the dust, but we had love for the person he used to be, so we just wasn't takin' him serious. Beyond that, it was just common knowledge to not loan him anything you expected to get paid back on.

So the nigga I was with puts my old buddy on the loudspeaker and motions for me to be quiet. Then we listen and laugh as ol' boy asks if they'd seen me around. Of course, the nigga told my old buddy he ain't seen me, even though I'm right there in his face takin' a one-on-one.

Then my old buddy makes a fool of himself by tellin' this dude that they ain't seen me because I'd been hidin' out. He told them I snitched on some shit that he never would specify, and a couple of weeks prior he had to call a shot on me, so the niggas at the tire shop stomped my teeth out on E. 14th, and now he was callin' to let these niggas know it's on sight when they see me.

What my old buddy didn't know is that I'd been with the people he was talkin' about me to every day for almost two weeks, and we was just at the tire shop earlier that same day.

When the fairytale phone call was over, the real hitter out of the two dudes I was with jokingly said to me, "Man-Man, I hear you tellin', Blood! Who you told on?"

I just lit my cigarette and cracked back at him with, "Shit, I thought you knew! I been tellin' on them niggas at the tire shop for knockin' all my teeth out!"

That's the only time I've ever seen the subject of snitchin' become a laughing matter. I mean, we laughed until we cried about that shit! Then we went back to the tire shop the next day and laughed again when we told them about it. But at no point did any of those dudes even almost think for a second that it was possible I could be a fuckin' snitch. And while ol' boy was in the house makin' phone calls, I was in the trenches makin' moves. So when his words were heard, my actions spoke for themselves. I didn't ever have to tell anyone I wasn't a snitch. And they knew for themselves that ain't nobody ever stomp my teeth out.

That's what stickin' to the G-Code will do for you. You'll be known for the kind of person you are, and nobody will ever be able to put dirt on your name. Because who you are as a man will always get you through. And whoever you happen to be, if you stay sturdy, the real will recognize you. You shall be judged by your actions in the street, so make sure to keep your steps solid.

Because the world is watching...

And the only thing that should ever come back when anybody runs a check on you, is the same kind of shit that would fit next to anybody else's name in this Game. The extra shit will happen and you'll do what a real one is supposed to. Don't be tryna do the most, just be yourself and do your best. And no matter how hard it may be, don't ever try to ease the pressure through the escape of some faulty shit.

Because there is no P without the G...

Remember that. And keep it as a major part – a guiding force – in your Ism.

VOYEURISM

Little Red Riding Hood: "Oh, what big eyes you have!" Big Bad Wolf: "All the better to see you with, my dear."

Voyeurism is often applied to some freaky shit that has to do with getting off on being a peeping Tom, or just having a mind that gets turned on by watching other people have sex. But it also applies to someone who enjoys watching the details of others. Especially private details. Point is, it's about watching – *closely* – especially when others don't think or know that you are, which is when they show their true selves. And that is what this principle means in the context that I use it here.

Remember, at all times, a pimp is supposed to employ the bonus lesson/principle of Game itself. And Game itself translates into tying everything together in order to maximize its usefulness; a play for every card in the deck. So for that reason, I will mix the two definitions of Voyeurism to explain this principle.

With that guideline in place, we can move on into how this Ism fits so importantly with pimpin'. Because I believe that there is more than one kind of intercourse people can engage in.

A lot of things about pimpin' consists of bypassing the overemphasis most people put on sexual things. Even if sex is a big part of your play, it's stupid to let it mean the same to you that it does to a trick or a square.

And so when we speak here of Voyeurism, we're going to apply it to intercourse while bypassing the sexual definition of intercourse.

In my humble opinion, deep conversations are the purest form of intercourse. Because if it's honest, the private things that are usually covered up, are shown. The same as if clothes are removed and bodies are revealed.

And when those personal thoughts are shared and put together in a conversation, it's no different than if private parts are helping each other reach climax. Except in this case, the climax is understanding.

To tackle it even further, if you can put a new idea into your ho's head, you just planted your seed. Same as her becoming pregnant. So every success and achievement is the birth of yet another baby.

Conversation is much more valuable and useful than sex, because you can employ it with more people. And in regards to Ism, you would do real good to pay close attention at all times to what people say. You should always be watching everybody for various reasons.

Pimps don't get the luxury of being overly involved with people. Not if they're really pimpin'. Because there should be no such thing as "gettin' lost in the moment" for a pimp. That's the only reason I allow myself to write books about pimpin' at all. Because no matter what I say, a non-pimp – a square – just won't get it. The reason for this is because the average person will not be able to achieve the required degree of disconnect.

Most people get lost in the moment.

I call it gettin' lost in the sauce...

The downfall of this weakness is being unable to pay enough attention to what's going on in your zone to know what or who you are dealing with. As a result, this person will not know how he should deal with the individual in question. Next thing you know, the hunter becomes the hunted, and the predator become prey.

But if Voyeurism is a principle, you're able to successfully employ, you will be able to watch another pimp accurately enough to see if he's a real pimp or not. That way you'll know if his hoes should/could become your hoes. This may be a possibility even if he's a real P, by the way. It'll also help you to spot potential prostitutes, and hoes that are open to being pulled onto your team.

Because you're watching what people do and how they move, you're seeing their results and all of what went into them getting those results. And in the process of paying attention, you remember what you hear or see, so that you have a pimp file on everyone you deal with. You know who's a crash dummy and who's just as smart as you are. You know who to ignore and who to listen to. More, and most importantly, you know how much to ignore and how much to listen to each person.

When I first got into this life, I thought every nigga who had a ho was a real pimp because I usually hung around people who were older than me. Then, after a little while of being down and around on some real things, other real things and people came into my life. Not necessarily "good" people in every instance, but for sure they were really from, and in, "the life."

Before I knew it, I was in a better and bigger pimp-type position than a few of the people I came into this Game looking up to. And as years went by, I left all those people so far behind, that I now don't even know how I ever even though they was pimps in the first place.

But before I got this extended understanding, I received my first clue as a gift. It came from my O.G. pimpin' potna Paul Tanner (R.I.P.). Everybody called him P. T., or pimpin' Paul. He was kind of gritty with it, but I respected him, and he was real cool. I say gritty because he wasn't really grimy – he could be trusted. But he was a pure enough pimp that he gave full consideration to how a grimy nigga would see things.

I bought my first old-school whip from P.T. It was a '72 Buick Skylark. He also had a clean-ass white Cadillac Eldorado Biarritz I wanted to buy from him, but I came up on a bitch he was tryna bag, and he never sold me the damn Caddy after that.

One day, after I had to let him know the bitch was now my bitch, we was in the Caddy drinkin' some Remy Martin. And in the process of choppin' up Game, I mentioned the name of a couple of people I thought were pimps. That's when P.T. told me the difference between a pimp and what these dudes were.

"My nigga, you green as fuck! And you still more of a pimp already than them muthafuckas gon' ever be," he said. "Those kinds of niggas make it hard on a real pimp because the bitch can run to one of them when she wanna get away from a real nigga like us."

I was confused because I knew these dudes, and their hoes sold pussy on a regular basis. They dressed nice, and the hoes had paid for the clothes. So what was I missin'? When I asked the question, P.T. clarified it for me.

"Man, how is it that you got hella money to spend on what you want, and them niggas don't? You already answered your own question. The hoes bought those clothes from them niggas. They not breakin' them bitches! They just them hoes boyfriends. That's why yo' young-ass come along and get three deep on 'em, and each one of them still stayed with only one ho apiece.

"Just because the hoes is real don't mean the niggas that got 'em is pimps, bruh. In reality, he don't got the bitch, the bitch got him. That's why you the only one with a chain. That's also why you the only one I see on the track every night. Because you the only one pimpin'."

Then I had to think back and remember that, when I got my chain and my rings, I was the only one buying things that day. Or any other day. And I had to admit that there really was a difference between what I was doing and what they was doing.

As my eyes opened up, a conversation I'd had with an older veteran ho came back to me. I had just told her that her daughter was about to be gettin' down for my crown. We were all in my car on our way to the track, and she told me point blank: "Man-Man, I ain't got no pimp, and I don't want my daughter to have no pimp either. When I got with my man, I chose him. He didn't knock me on the track, and I don't give him my money. But I got his back because I'm a real bitch."

I thought she was drunk and just talkin' out the side of her neck. I had love for her, so I wasn't gonna repeat what she'd said to her "boyfriend." That might get her beat up.

But now with what P.T. had just told me, it all made more sense. Because Mama Linda hung out with these other hoes me and P.T. were discussing.

That's when I started really paying attention to the people I interacted with. That's when I learned to spot the many different levels of this Game. That's when I recognized the difference between the talkers and the walkers.

Because everybody don't walk it like they talk it.

But conversations are just as crucial as observing a person's steps. Because if you remember not to get lost in the moment, you can spot patterns over time. So even if a person is lying to make themselves look better than they are, certain details will still reveal the truth.

Remember, two plus two equals four. So when shit don't add up, something is wrong. But at the same time, there are also things that should never add up. And when you see this, there's something wrong there, too. Because Game itself shows you how to read and play every card that comes your way.

I remember later on in life, I was in jail and ended up knockin' one of the chicks who worked there. I don't want the bitch to lose her job, so I won't give up too much info on the surrounding circumstances. Let's just say that for about a year and a half of my life, she was my bitch. Not my ho, though; just a bonus in a bad situation. More like a girlfriend who would feel disrespected by the word "bitch."

Now, what should've been a red flag to begin with was how this muthafucka went on her way to put herself in my path. I say this because anyone paying critical attention would conclude from the fact that the outside world wasn't being too nice to this chick. But anyone who can't find what they want in the free world is a flawed person. There are just too many choices out there for anyone to draw a blank like that.

So one of my more Voyeuristic activities, whenever I meet a new chick on any level, is to get as much of her backstory as possible. Usually this will show patterns that help a pimp see what it is with a bitch. But sometimes you'll see one thing and miss another. And other times you won't yet know that you're dealing with an undesirable person, so when they lie you won't catch it right away, because you're too busy feelin' yourself.

Anyway, the backstory on this individual was one that told of all men letting her down, and most of her friends doing the same – blah, blah, blah...

So I'm thinkin', *Oh, once she gets a muthafucka to be real, she'll be fine. She just been havin' goofballs.*

I never had to tell her I was a pimp. She had access to my file, so she knew. And it seemed to fascinate her. So the angle I used was experimental. As long as my principles were upheld, I could compromise my process. My bottom line was to win in the end.

So, one day, she asked what I would do besides pimp, and I told her I would open a business. Maybe a pizza joint, or something. Then I told her she don't gotta buy me a 'Benz, just buy me a pizza joint so I could buy us both 'Benzes.

The craziest part about all of this is that I was dead serious. I wasn't tryna get over on her at all. And the response she gave me was, "I got you."

So in other conversations she said little things that made me ask a couple of key questions. One of the questions was, "Hey, are you one of those Me-Too movement kind of bitches who think, no matter what, they just have to play against a man just to prove a point?"

She laughed and said, "Hell no. They're ridiculous with some of their issues."

My other question was: "Hey, I've had bitches with your same zodiac sign before. All them hoes switched up on me out the blue. Is that what you're gonna do, too?"

"Oh, I'm not that kind," she said. "I'm actually the opposite of that. Thing about me is, I'm loyal to a fault."

Let's just pause the story right there so I can point out a very obvious and important point in this lesson.

I didn't pull those questions out of my ass! I am who I am, and that includes being what I am at all times. So when she spoke, I listened close enough to develop these concerns. I watched how she moved, as well.

She constantly complained about male co-workers, and always made references to men as if they were some separate species or on some opposing team. So I was definitely watching her like I was supposed to. And I think I can say I was watching myself, because I made no mistakes pullin' this chick into my mix.

But even though I spotted what was rotten about her, my surrounding situation was even worse. I was down the highway in another state, locked up. This put me at the mercy of the local women whose definition of being real didn't match up with my own. So if the position my life was in at that moment had me wearing Levi's and cheap tennis shoes every day, it's safe to say I was a million miles away from being able to do what I wanted to do, right?

Therefore, being able to do the same thing daily with this chick that I needed a visit once a week to achieve otherwise was a powerful distraction. Especially when my visitor was really starting to let me down at that particular moment, when I met this particular chick.

My conclusion is that being in a bad position made me sell my soul for a jelly roll.

The Bible says something to the effect of when a person is already full, even honey ain't sweet. But when you're starving, even bitter things tatse sweet. And my pimpin' was so starved for some stimulation, the bitter bitch tasted real sweet for a little while there.

But even though I looked both ways before I crossed the street, I still forgot to observe the street itself. A pimp can't only watch himself and other people; the surrounding

87

situation must also be considered. Would that bitch have fucked with me if we had met outside of the place we met? Would I have fucked with her? Certain hoes would've never gotten in the door if I was already havin' money when I met them. And some regular bitches would've never got in the door with me if I was already havin' hoes.

In his book, *How to Hustle & Win: Sex, Money, Murder Edition*, King Guru spoke all about emotional manipulators. That shit really exists! I call 'em crash dummies and vampires. They fuck everything up and feed off draining you of your positive energy. They usually thrive on chaos and sabotage and don't hang around long when things get good. The move they'll make in those circumstances will be to either run off, or wreck what is going so well, because they're most comfortable in mystery.

Voyeurism is the principle that peeps possibility. Both good and bad. So in the same way you can use it to catch a potentially profitable situation, you can and must also use it to catch a potentially harmful situation.

Watch your homies, watch your potnas, watch yourself, watch your hoes. Watch, watch, watch! Watch your step, watch your circumstance and situation – watch it all, at *all* times!

I was talkin' to my son's mama the other day and she told me that, even if my lil man didn't look like me, she would know he was my son because he got his little ways – where he acts and does things that she knows he got from me.

When I asked her what she meant, the examples she gave were in the way he might spazz out, and then get right back to whatever he was doing before he flashed. Her other example was the way he sits still and watches everything, listens to everything, and knows everything. He doesn't ask many questions. Instead, he pays attentions and sees for himself.

And this is at five years old...

I guess I'm a pretty good stud if my pups come out acting just like me, huh? Too bad ol' girl don't realize that some of the things he does, shows me without anybody having to tell me, exactly what kind of things my lil man has seen and heard with her. If she knew better she might do better, but first she would have to learn how to watch her own self. Then she could understand how to watch other people before she let them into her life, instead of after it's too late. That way, the only people that ever got close enough to show her son anything would be the kind who only showed him good things.

Me and my son's mom did OK for three months in three different states until she decided to let jealousy and pregnancy concerns make her leave. My son is a real product of this Game. And I often wonder what other things will come naturally to him, because I know how he was bred. If anybody on this planet can say he was born to Mack, it would be him, for sure. But I can only hope he doesn't get snagged up in the street life.

Of course, I'll be watching, so he'll have the best guidance he can get. It's just a question of what he listens to. Because the bad part about having kids in the Game is that you leave them scattered all over the place. And I was national wit' it, so we're talkin' about multiple time zones from coast to coast.

That's another thing you'll one day see when you start to really look. The same thing that makes you laugh will make you cry...

Anyway, my point if that, is a five-year-old with real pimp instinct running heavy in his blood has sense enough to use Voyeurism, so should everybody else who claims to have any real Game.

If I would've watched ol' girl in the jailhouse situation, I would've seen the things I prefer to separate myself from. And in the end, when those things showed themselves, I did end up separating myself.

Voyeurism will let you know if your plan for someone is a match for their identity. Because what you want will not always be who or what they are.

Even though this principle is priceless in many ways, its highest value is in combination with the principle of Separatism, because it gives you a kind of x-ray vision after a while. This helps you see through the many disguises people will wear to cover up who they really are. And that can make the difference between being able to move on, or not being able to make another move ever again. So don't sleep on how important it is to peep Game on people, places, and circumstances, because the law of the jungle has no regard to if you understand it or not.

Let's look closer at that part for a moment.

There can be serious consequences to not using the principle of Voyeurism in your program. Energy is just a real as air. You can't see it, but you can feel it, and it has a very real effect on everybody's life. There's no exception to this rule. I've seen my money change according to the kind of energy I allowed to exist in my life. And that energy was directly connected to what kind of hype the person in my life was on. That boils down to what kind of person I allowed into my life. Good people on a good hype brought good results; bad people on a bad hype brought bad results.

This aspect of Voyeurism is so real, that upon getting rid of a bad-vibe-bringing individual, I immediately went back to seeing my money grow after it had been on a very noticeable standstill.

I stopped being a square a very long time ago. So I'm not the type who gets too far into making a woman feel like she's doing me a favor by fuckin' with me. For this reason, I'm usually the one who says "yes" or "no" about if we're going to be involved or not. And I try not to leave too many women with too many regrets. It's very rare that I will ever find myself with no other options when I reach the end of a relationship. But when I look back on the last relationship I pumped the brakes on, I almost want to fall to my knees and thank God for making me a real one. Because I promise, a regular square-ass dude would've been wrecked on the side of the road after that kind of an assault on his livelihood.

I am still, and always will be, a human being. And by human nature, we often fall short of perfection. Pimpin' doesn't make you perfect. It's just a mindset that works constructively with other people's imperfections.

Many times, the Mack in me was my only saving grace. And knowing how to play my hand is what did the rest, once I'd managed to sidestep a potentially destructive outcome.

With that being said, I must admit that I'm not immune to a mad move on my part being a bad move on my pimpin'. So when my work made me mad at her for not sockin' it to my pocket the way she was supposed to, I cut her off like I was supposed to.

But I was only lookin' at that one faulty episode of financial exchange. In the process, I wasn't paying any attention to the additional fact that my pockets were fat because of this same individual.

Voyeurism at its best should make you watch and see everything. But human emotion made me shrink-wrap my vision around what had me upset.

In my own defense, I must share the fact that it was her fault. I've got one pet peeve, and that is lying. I hate to be lied to. Because when my expectations are not met, my time is wasted, when I could have been off making shit happen some other way.

But, if this scripture is to be authentic, I must also tell you that there's no defense for overlooking pimp protocol. So much so that the Game will usually give me a little bite whenever I don't respect that protocol.

The fact is that I knew this individual was predisposed to shoot herself in the foot. So when she made the bad move, I should have just pimped past it. Instead, I dropped her and replaced her just to prove to myself that I could. And that might have been OK if I had not done it out of anger, because my emotion made me not look closely enough at her replacement before I put her in the mix. And that replacement would've never got in my business under normal circumstances.

The rest of the truth is that the energy of this replacement struggled to kill my vibe as soon as she felt secure enough to do her dance. When I saw she was an undercover destroyer of good things, I dismissed her. But if I wasn't who I am, I wouldn't have been able to bounce right back to what I was doing before she stepped into my world.

Ultimately, the only setback I suffered was a waste of time. But time is money to a man like me, so I should have moved better than that, because if I wasn't a real money manager, I would have gone broke. And if I wasn't a real money magnet, I wouldn't have been able to put myself back to where I was when I made this bad decision. And if I wasn't a real Mack, I wouldn't have got that old bitch back.

So thank God I'm me and not your everyday average square, or that bitch would have been the false hope that made me flush my Ism down the toilet.

Furthermore, flush or no flush, another muthafucka wouldn't have been able to bounce back. But thanks to my Ism, I played my hand in a way that made it possible for me no matter what else I ever do, because I'm more committed to the guidelines I live by then I'll ever be to some new addition to my life. People come and go a lot more often than you come across the good ones who stick around, so if you don't stand for something, you'll fall for anything – even fake things that don't add up, or harmful things you need to avoid.

Keeping your eye on the prize goes hand in hand with keeping your mind on your principles. It's like a second sight that will steer you past problems your physical vision might miss.

That's Voyeurism: Watching intercourse as it occurs. Even when you're part of the show. You're the director and the audience all at once; you run the show and watch the play, all at the same time.

In conjunction with other aspects of the other principles that you stick to, Voyeurism is the basic beginning to every useful idea you have.

If you're playing chess, you watch what moves your opponent makes to decide what you'll do next. And in a card Game, you'll watch what cards the other player or players play to know how to go about playin' your hand. You can't play at all without some way of seeing what's going on. And winning with your eyes closed is impossible! So be watchful in your interactions. And then watch the people you interact with when they interact with others. After that, compare their interaction to the other people's interactions and pay attention to what you feel.

In the end, your Ism will direct your steps according to what you have seen, with not only your eyes, but also your ears and your mind.

Putting yourself in a position to always see clearly is the bottom line of Voyeurism. That way you're not driving blind with no idea of where you want to go. Because staying on top of your Game is what having any Game at all is all about.

REALISM

"Have heart, have money."

– Old Street Saying

This particular principle of Ism is probably the most important of all, if you have to choose a single one. I say this because if all the other principles were steps on a journey, then Realism would count as the destination.

It is the conclusion to the conversation of what kind of checklist anyone should use when dealing with other people, and this is especially so for a pimp.

As I progressed through this life, I graduated from being in it just to be in it, to being in it to look good. Then I got to the level where I was in it to win it as a way to survive.

For some people, who have the wrong understanding of what survival means, a real-life situation will justify doing foul and scandalous things to get over on other people. But for a real individual, I would say that what such a situation really calls for is your play to not only be successful, but to be repeated as many times as possible. You can't live on only one meal, so you cannot burn all of your bridges on only one play.

The bottom line is closely related to the principle of Socialism. Don't do people dirty, because their outcome is as important as your own. If they're on your team, then your outcomes are all connected.

All kinds of things can and do take place in the jungle of this life we live. This is true. And of course, we will do what we must – but not against the team, though. We must either keep it real, or make sure it ends up real in the end, because if we don't keep Realism in our program, our program won't last long at all. And unfortunately, there have been a lot of good providers out there who kept it solid for the wrong person, and now will remain renegades, or just went to waste as a result of their folks not being real.

Even if your intentions are good, you must remember to do your best to extend that goodness to the results you give to your folks. In this way, the principle of Realism applies to both pimp and hoes. You can never be a good one if you're not a real one. And you can never be a real one if your truth has no proof. So make sure there are things to show in life that exist because you're in the mix.

There was a time in my youth when every time I brought my folks around my old buddy to show off my Game, he was never impressed. I couldn't understand this because the little chick was a real cute mixed girl with long pretty hair and big titties. Plus she was a go-getter beyond compare who stayed through a few trips down the highway.

I didn't know how to form the question I had on my mind, so I waited until my buddy got around to sharing his thoughts. I was afraid he knew something about ol' girl that he'd heard in the street. But what it turned out to be was that he never saw her nails done, and he couldn't understand why this was the case.

So one day I got a call from him on the phone. He said, "Hey man, I gotta know this. How is you gettin' away with not doin' lil mama's nails and shit?"

"Awwww, man, big bruh... I ain't trippin' off that shit, so she ain't trippin' either," I said without knowing how stupid I sounded.

He then paused and took a deep breath as if he was patiently talking to a child. Then he taught me a lesson I never forgot.

"Look, man, you can't be out here sendin' yo' bitch around a bunch of other hoes lookin' shabby. That's some basic shit a bitch 'posed to get.

"How would you feel if you had to tell me you couldn't afford to go to the barbershop? That's embarrassing to even think about.

"Just because she don't know no better don't mean you ain't 'posed to do it. That make you look bad. You gotta do a bitch better than that when she break you off the way that one been doin'. Or else that bitch can't even say she winnin' by fuckin' with you."

I thought about what he said very seriously. This particular buddy was my potna's father and he had been ballin' for years on every level of the Game. All over the city of Richmond, the name Johnny Simon is recognized in attachment to wisdom and success in the street, so I'd be an idiot to ignore his advice.

Needless to say, I began takin' my folks to get her nails done, and her whole little vibe started to sparkle with a new level of excitement.

It was clear to see that she felt like we were getting somewhere. And that got me into dressing my peoples up to make sure they looked official at all times. There's a whole other level of joy that comes into your atmosphere when the results of Realism become part of your scenario.

The first time I sent a ho on automatic, I was in Virginia with plans to hit New Jersey that weekend. But I had some things I'd bought online that were due for a delivery and yet to arrive when it was time to go. So what I did was send my work to New Jersey on her own while I waited in Virginia for my package to arrive. We stayed in touch until I caught back up with her in New Jersey. I kept my word about coming, and she kept her word about gettin' paid. This led to a long run of successful trips, because we discovered we could trust each other to give what was expected.

Those real results even left a residue of achievement that was so potent, it attracted other hoes to replace that one once we parted company. The pictures of those times and the trophies they gave me, removed all doubt from the minds of future hoes to come, because they could see the Realism, and that was enough to prove what I said could really happen.

There's a lot to be said for the principle of Realism if you plan to win. Because fake shit don't last. And anyone who runs out of plays in any Game is going to lose. That means, if your situation isn't based on something that can be repeated or scrutinized closely, it won't continue. So don't settle for the shortcut of bullshitting your was through life.

It's true that sometimes you might have to fake it to make it. But that's not the same as bullshitting your way through. That's the act of bullshitting your way into something, then once you get in the door, your Realism should take you the rest of the way.

I once ran into a real good ho who'd already had too many bad results by the time she met me. She was dead set against havin' a pimp in her life and said so soon after we started talking. I knew that she'd never had a real pimp before, but she didn't know. I also knew that what she was really done with was having her money and her time wasted more than she was done with pimps. But she didn't know this, either.

But why would she listen to me when we'd just met? And why would I argue with her, when her mind was made up?

So I must admit, I told this individual a very good lie to get her to give me a few thousand dollars. Actually, more like twenty thousand dollars within a month. But in that month, I fucked with that ho the right way and saved every bit of her money. I didn't play her out of anything except an opportunity to show her that I was real. And when we reached that twenty-stacks, I showed it to her. I also told her I wasn't really gonna do what I said at first, but then we enjoyed that money together and added to it. And when I asked her if she'd ever touched racks like that on her own, she admitted she hadn't. Truth was that, she didn't even know she could.

Our mutual appreciation carried us through many months of getting that kind of money together. She wasn't mad at the lie I told, because it was outweighed by the truth I proved. So in the end, Realism got me through. But if I would've ran off with that twenty of kept tryna be dishonest, I would've missed all the other twenty-stack months she gave me. I'm talkin' about three years' worth of twenty-thousand-dollar months.

You do the math...

Realism is the end Game to the play of every other one of the principles of Ism. Or at least it should be. And having your mind tuned into that frequency, you will spot fake shit easier. Because it won't match up with what you know you're on. In the long run, it'll avoid a whole lot of trouble.

There was one time when I first got up into the New York, New Jersey area that my taste for Realism saved me. I had a bad lil Latina girl who was posting up ads with some real impressive pics. I had her with a lot of jewelry and a mink coat in expensive rooms, so anybody who saw her would surely connect her to a very worthwhile situation. But my peoples Big Johnny had already warned me about how the undercover police activity was more in depth and sophisticated on the east coast, so I had my folks under instructions to be careful.

As the days went by, I got comfortable and went to feelin' myself. And before long, Big Johnny's advice was no longer in the front of my mind. But he taught me well, though, so the overall rule of Realism never fell out of place. Therefore, when an attractive Puerto Rican chick hit my folks up to give her props on her pics, I just kicked back and watched the situation. Pretty soon the conversation went from the pics into the impressive details; compliments on my provider's jewelry, and real respect for her mink coat.

By stroking our ego so much, this random chick had me and my folks not even suspicious in any major way. And to be honest, we thought we was about to bag us a bad bitch from the Bronx.

So when ol' girl started crackin' at baby about how she must be up under a helluva P, my only response was to start crackin' back. But my Socialism made me keep my bitch in play, so I only relayed messages through her at first. And my Activism made me employ the principle of Voyeurism to keep watching this bitch's words. This made me keep all communication on my ho's phone, even when the prospective chick asked for my phone number. That was the principle of Separatism.

Then, when she asked for a picture of me, I told her that the way her future looked was more important than how I looked. So I sent her pics of my home's living room and bedrooms. I sent her pics of big money all rubber-banded up. I sent her pics of the leather and woodgrain interior of my car. But none of me. This was Mysticism at work, being employed with a healthy dose of Separatism.

Because she couldn't call me and she couldn't see me, she was separated from that privilege until she was at least talkin' about payin' me.

But the whole time, there was some unclear quality that seemed to be missing from this chick's conversation. Or maybe some part of her conversation just remained unexplainably unclear. I couldn't put my finger on it, but ol' girl didn't check out all the way on my pimp radar, so I kept crackin' at her, but didn't put too much on it. But my Activism kicked into gear based on me thinking I was about to bag me a New York bitch, so of course it wasn't long before I ended up workin' on gettin' myself another lil piece of Puerto Rican work from the Bronx. And now I could take what this other chick was talkin' about, and with the new one, have somethin' to compare it with.

How could it not add up when they was both Puerto Rican chicks from the Bronx, right? When I combine my Socialism with my Voyeurism, I should see some similarities between what each one said.

At least, that would be the case, if each one of these women were as they should be...

But I was in an old jungle that was brand-new to me, so of course the predators were sniffing around to see if they could knock me off.

What happened was the mixing up of similarity between what the first chick said and what the second chick said about the Game in that part of the country. The second one sounded more official, but that didn't add up because the first one was older. So what I did was bet all my chips on Realism to see what a local would think about my dilemma.

The only local I knew was the second chick from the Bronx, so I said "fuck it" and ran the whole situation down to her about the other chick. I wanted her opinion hella bad because by now the first chick was tryna choose up.

When I got done exposing myself, I had completely scrambled my damn play with lil mama who was official, but she did tell me what I needed to know, though.

"Whoever that bitch is, you better ask more questions or find another way to get yo' answers. That shit don't sound right," she said cautiously.

So my next move was to look for ol' girl's ad on Back Page to see where she been gettin' money. Then, when she gave me the excuses about not puttin' pics on her ad, I tried to backtrack her phone number. That should've given me every ad she'd ever put up on Back Page with the same number, as well as any links to other sites.

Still, no luck. So now I know this ain't no ho.

Google to the rescue at that point. And as soon as I put the search on that phone number, I got linked to a website of some multi-jurisdictional organization that works hand in hand with law enforcement. The shit was so crazy, I ran the Google search on that same phone number about five more times! I couldn't believe it. Here I was, politely pimpin' in my own lane, and these muthafuckas was aggressively tryna snag me up.

Of course, I cut ol' girl off and changed my folk's phone number. That's when I realized I was slippin' by havin' the Las Vegas number on an ad in New York. That let everybody in the area know I had just traveled coast to coast. And for law enforcement, that put me on the radar as a sex trafficker.

If my Realism wasn't tuned in on some real shit, I might've fallen into that trap. Real recognizes real, so that fake shit didn't smell right. And then really bein' on some pimpish pursuits, I was at another bitch who helped me see what was going on. So that whole scenario would only have worked on somebody who don't really do this. Which makes me thank God I do this for real, because there really ain't no such thing as a lucky star. And a falling star is like a sinking ship, to me, so why would I wish on some shit like that? Think about it; it's falling down! Do you wanna fall down, too? I'd much rather invest me faith, energy, and hopes into something that stands up against whatever forces may try to pull me down.

I read a book back in the day by Donald Goines called *Whoreson*, about the son of a whore. And in that book, the mother had a plan to turn her son into a pimp. Throughout his whole young life, she put him up under all the other kind of players around Detroit – professional gamblers, conmen, and gangsters were who raised Whoreson.

Somewhere along the line, the question was asked of the ho about why she was exposing her son to all these other things if a pimp is what he was going to be Her response was that, in order to be a real pimp, he would have to be a complete man first.

Imagine that...

The book started with her being pregnant, but still having to get money because her faulty pimp had left her. So she clearly had a reason to question the Ism. Then, as a trick was eating her pussy, her water broke in his face. Nasty. So she obviously wasn't lookin' at a customer with any respect. And since the customer gave her a bad reaction, she was not too fond of the male species at the moment she realized she'd spit out a male child, so she named him Whoreson, and said if he was ashamed of what is mama was, then fuck him, too! It was a cold lil book that told a story taking place in the Game on the streets of Detroit.

To be honest, I didn't really identify with it, but there were still bits and pieces that stayed with me, and I always wondered why that was. The part of the story I shared above is one of the ones that stayed with me.

After reading countless other books, living a little more of my life, then finally writing a few books of my own, I finally understood why that part of the story stayed with me. It's because it showed the ho's mindset. Even if it was extreme, it showed what a ho might go through, and the effects it could have.

Any real individual will be the kind of person who pays attention to why people do what they do. This knowledge will always give you insight towards understanding aspects of your play that other people will overlook.

It can be truthfully said that I've been a mean muthafucka in my lifetime. But it's so much easier to be a beast than it is to be a man, so to be honest, I was taking shortcuts into the realm of Realism at the times I chose the smashy-bo route. And the more I gained in experience, the less I could deny the truth.

I also have a mind that has a memory. And when I look back on some of my mean moments, I regret the moves I made.

Realism is the coin of regret. Like all coins, it has two sides. One side is your own regret; the other side is the regret you've caused someone else to feel. It's the only currency a pimp won't want a whole lot of. But it's good to have at least a little bit so you can steer clear of what earned you that coin. Then your application of Game itself will make you put a spin on your Realism that steers you into avoiding that kind of regret. It's like the fuel that will make your Ism go to a good place instead of a bad one. Because the remembrance of those regrets will make you give birth to better results.

I remember I had a ho from the Central Valley part of California. She was the first girl I ever went to Las Vegas with. But before we got there, she flipped my car over when I let her drive us through the desert. Needless to say, once we got a rental and made it the rest of the way, I wasn't in the best of moods.

I could've pimped up on another car if I would've just looked beyond how mad I was, but instead, my bad attitude got a bad reaction from her and we parted company in Arizona. But I did it cordially, though. I drove her ass right to the airport and dropped her off to go on about her business. However, I had told her I was going to win, and I meant it, so I stayed down for my crown.

The regret of letting myself push a willing participant away made me check myself as time went by. A couple of years later, I came across that same individual again while I was in a winning position. When baby saw that I had two cars and a house out of the same Game she'd decided to leave behind, she had to face the regret of leaving me. The next thing she did was leave her boyfriend, quit her job, and brought her ass back to me. She went on to help buy me three more cars and a Rolex watch, on top of keeping my bankroll in the five-figure area for the whole time I had her.

She'd probably still be around if my number one had not seen her as a threat to whatever agenda she had. But what I can say for sure is that Realism is what brought her back to me. It was the consciousness of what mindset I would inspire in a woman who put herself into my program. It was the concern about if I would be anything more than a bad memory. It was the Realism that made me stay on track even when I was not on stage. That's what brought ol' girl back. Because the remembrance of regret gave birth to respectable results. So respectable results are another part of the Realism principle. They are not the coin, though. They are what the coin should be used to pay for.

Because if regret doesn't inspire better results, it will inspire bad results. And the choice is yours regarding which one you choose to purchase once the coin is in your possession.

You can see regrets in your past and avoid repeating the mistake that caused them, or you can see the possibility of regret ahead of you and avoid it before it comes. You can remember times where you must admit that you inspired regret and do better next time, or you can look at a situation you're faced with and decide not to inspire any future regrets.

These are the mechanics of Realism. Or rather they are the mechanical breakdown on how Realism should work. But if you're too fake to admit your mistakes, you'll never be able to properly use Realism to your full advantage.

And even if you don't care how anybody else feels, you still gotta treat people how you want to be treated. Or you can't ever really claim to be real. And if you're not really real, how can you really expect anyone on your team to be?

I said earlier that Realism was the "mechanical breakdown" of your Ism. And everything mechanical boils down to mathematical precision. This doesn't mean you need to be stressed out on precision, but the math part is worth paying attention to, because when things don't add up, they're usually not real. And when you add bad habits with bad moves, it'll usually equal bad results. And since numbers don't lie, math is the only language that always tells the truth. You can never get what you want without putting enough into it, because shortcakes don't make long bread. And small cows don't make big steaks. Two plus two equals four. You'll never get it by adding two plus one. So don't try to get away with not doing enough. This goes for what you accept as well as for what you deliver.

That's the philosophy behind Realism... *Real Ism!*

CONCLUSION

The many avenues of Ism are like the stars in the sky. You cannot count all the possible ways you can twist and tangle potential applications. But hopefully with documenting these seven basics, I have established at least the foundation. From there, any real one can build the structure of his own individual variation.

You may have noticed that in the description of one principle I mentioned how it related to another, or led me to another when applying it properly. The fact is, a few of these principles could've been shared under the same label, but that would've been an incomplete representation, because some things need to be recognized or employed in a certain order, or on their own individual merits. So, I introduced them as I did, regardless of what was possible.

Anything repeated was important enough to say more than once. So, I hope as the reader, you'll zoom in on these things and allow them to work double- or triple-time toward you retaining the information.

And always remember this: Prostitution is a hustle that gave birth to Pimpin'. But pimpin is not what defines Ism. Even though the lifestyle invented the term as we use it, the concept itself has been mastered in many ways.

Pimpin' takes the potential of a good, worthwhile prostitute and maximizes that potential. Without that prostitute, I don't think he should be technically calling himself a pimp. But I understand why this is something he still might do, though. Because the concept of Ism may still be in whatever process he's employing to gain his success. So that, even though it's a different body if the hustle itself is not prostitution, the same spirit prevails – the spirit of Ism.

Because Ism is universal.

And in the same way that *The Art of War* is taught in corporate training camps to help prospective executives win in business, my principles of Ism can be used by anyone who wishes to win at whatever they do. Don't let the subject make you miss the substance of the rules that I live by. I didn't share them for the sole purpose of perpetuating a society of pimps. My goal was, and always is, to introduce the proper context of the mindset behind pimpin'. To dislodge some of the stereotype, and sow seeds of increased possibility among those who participate in the sport. For hoes to know that there's a better kind of pimp, and for pimps to know there's a better way. So that both may one day discover a better hustle, or at least make a bigger hustle out of the one they've chosen.

That is my eternal aim. Because whether the world wants to know it or not, many of us are just people trying to make it. And a society that envies us, blames us, or is ashamed of using our services, misrepresents us as some subhuman species of people unworthy of any kind of respectable recognition. And without my effort, many of us may slip into believing the worse scenario about who we are, or what we can be. And that's bullshit, because I know better.

We're not stuck. We can grow and graduate into bigger and better things! We're not cursed! We can climb our way out of present circumstances with a more constructive situation! And we're not bound to drown unless we choose not to swim!

That said, don't let mainstream media mislead you into thinking less of yourself or those on your team by looking down on whatever moves are being made. Take pride in yourself at all times, and make up your mind to get somewhere worthwhile in life with whatever you do.

This is only the beginning of what the application of Ism can make possible for you...

7 PIMP PRICIPLES

YOU GOTTA LIKE WHO LIKES YOU

"They pay you to pay attention."
– Pimpin Ken

In every aspect of life there will always be different strokes for different folks. But at certain basic levels, some things will remain the same no matter what.

For me, one of those things is that I like who likes me. And that's how I choose who to get into a groove with when it really comes down to it. But what can be different about this guideline, in spite of my steadfast observance of it, is how it applies from person to person. Because the science of this segment sits on what it means to each individual involved.

The first key to understanding words is to know what they mean, but in this Game, it's better to know how the word is being used. That's the number one step in learning anything from what someone says. So at all times, it is critical to remember that everything said in these segments will be spoken from a pro-pimpin' perspective.

With that in mind, we must face the fact that what might be beautiful to the average individual will usually be ugly if you apply it to some Ism. So, before we get lost in translation, let's define the word "like."

Since the proof is the truth is all aspects of Ism-based interests, there is no part of pimpin' that can ever be considered as anything real without the good results outweighing the bad results. Therefore, I think it's safe to say that if someone likes you, they should be tryna increase the goodness in your life.

You can't share the same vision with someone who doesn't speak the same language as you do because you'll both be lookin' in opposite directions and disagree on what the destination should be. So, the first part of liking who likes you is to get down with who gets down like you do. Vibe with your tribe. That way their understanding of what it means to "like you" doesn't clash with what you need a person who likes you to do.

It's cool to be able to like the person you're teamed up with in this hustle, but it's much more important that they like you. Because as a pimp, you're not in it for social enjoyment, you're in it to get paid. And whoever "likes" you the most will be the one who pays you the most. Period. Anything less is some anti-pimpin' type of outlook that should not apply to your Ism.

I say this because this belief is a safeguard against the trap of getting sidetracked by predatory intentions on the part of the wrong teammate.

A pretty girl who rocks your world in the bedroom may one day come along and kill your career by using "love" against you if you allow it. All it takes is for you to let non-profitable values make you forget to judge her more by what she brings to your table than how she claims to feel about you.

So, when I like who likes me, I'm remembering that it ain't the beauty, it's the duty. That means I must run away from one who says she loves me if she thinks "love" means we're supposed to run each other in circles and claim our

Game is the best without ever doin' anything to really get the best result out of it.

If she likes me, she wants me to have the most, and the best, because she takes the same pride in the appearance of my program as she does in her own personal appearance.

And my appreciation makes it worth her while because I'll like her in the same way. That's the definition of a real deal, in which you will both prosper.

Being a real hardhead from way back, I had to get it wrong a few times before I knew for sure what getting it right was all about. So don't think for a single second that pimp sense just shines down from ho heaven upon a chosen few. Because when it comes down to worldly wisdom, we usually gotta go through it to get to it. And pain of some sort is what makes the brain grow smarter in ways that are not forgotten. There are not many exceptions to his rule.

A common mistake a lot of people in general will make is to jump right out of the ashes of a bad situation into something new. It's like they have a need to prove that the old situation was not the only thing they could get. And it will usually turn out to be that whatever gets jumped into ends up being something they should've avoided.

So, at a time when I wanted to prove to myself and everybody else that I could knock a bad bitch, I exchanged numbers with a little renegade named Sensation. She was high yellow, like a light-bright or damn near white, with big titties, a beautiful smile, and pretty hair. Her eyes were somewhere between being blue and green, and it was clear that she'd seen enough to have a lot of Game about herself. But the best thing about her was how much she "liked" me.

When I called her, she came wit' it and paid me enough to make me feel like a P. When I popped up on her unexpectedly, she would drop whatever she was doin' to make herself available to me. I was always proud to show her off because she was so damned pretty, and once she caught onto this, she never failed to put on extras to make me look like a boss.

But what I wasn't understanding yet was that she thrived on the attention more than she did on being with me. It was about the partying with her, and if that didn't outweigh the hustle, she would lose interest. So she could never really make anything happen for me because she wasn't really tryna win for herself. As a result, we were only an item for as long as I was lost in the medication of riding around the Bay Area with my music turned up loud blowing purple clouds and playin' wit' my nose.

I can't even say how we fell apart, because she never officially left me, and nobody ever called to serve me any news about her choosin' up. My own natural attraction to gettin' money just made it grind time, so I slowed down on all the social activity. And two or three hoes down the line, I realized I wasn't around Sensation as much now that the financially-focused part of the Game was on my mind.

It's crucial to always be doin' the math when you're navigating your way through the hoes you meet in these streets. Because as I look back on that, it's easy to see how a lesser experienced or lesser dedicated man could get stuck on stupid with a bitch like that. Because Sensation did enough to fit herself into my life, but not enough to improve it. So regardless of what we could technically call it, in the end, my results would have revealed a stand-still or a shrinking of my bankroll's growing ability.

When hoes ran off on me, or tried to sabotage my Ism, my money suffered until I found a solution. So, should I still be sayin' Sensation liked me? Or did she actually hate me without knowing it? I think the real question should be this: If it all looks the same, why not treat it the same?

If I can't tell the difference between your liking me and hating on me when I look at what you're doing, I'm not going to tell myself I can win with you around. So, if I'm tryna win, then a person like that cannot be a part of my plan.

Separate yourself from what doesn't add to your growth when it comes to the hoes you accept into your program.

The other part of this guideline is the more obvious one. You don't ever want to go after what catches your eye and pick the "privilege" of having her over another chick who is really tryna be on your team. Because the one who's trying is the one who likes you for real, and she's the one who will bring you up when you're down.

On the other hand, the one you're chasing after is going to feel like she did you some kind of favor by getting with you. That will usually turn into her thinking or acting like you owe her something, and that's a one-way ticket to not getting paid. So, if you want to win in the pimp Game for real, you must learn to like who likes you.

This hustle has pitfalls just like any other life journey anyone can ever experience. One of the most dangerous, in my opinion, is to get yourself caught up with trying to impress other pimps or people on the sidelines.

I've seen potential players go broke on a car or some jewelry when they didn't even have a stable place to live. And sitting quietly in the background with a broken spirit was the ho who worked hard and only got a dose of disappointment for her troubles.

But that kind of mistake can also cross over into the hoes you choose. Because some dudes will pass up a real deal just because he only wants to be seen with "bad bitches." This can be a bad choice if bad results come along with those bad bitches. Keeping up with the Kardashians will land you in the loser's circle if you let looks decide which partner to pick.

A pimp's pockets are the only thing that should determine the decisions he makes.

So "looking like she can get it" is never better than being the one who actually wants to get it for you. Profit beats potential every time. And then you must make sure that you know what it means for a ho to like you so you don't get fooled into paying valuable attention to a worthless waste of your time.

LET A HO BE A HO

"If I ever go broke, I'll just break hoes."
— Too $hort

One thing that counts as an unbreakable rule of this Game is the saying about not turning hoes into housewives. I've personally done enough research on the subject to say that anyone who ignores this rule will be miserable in the end.

But of course, we will always remember that nobody in the Game got into it because they were about following any rules. And there's nothing wrong with rule breaking, as long as the rule is still understood well enough to benefit from their moral value whether you obey the instruction or not. However, most will not achieve enough experience, or listen to enough advice to really learn how to do this.

Some good examples I saw along the way on my path to enlightenment were pimps like Gangster Brown, Dr. Silk, and Rosebud, who all did the most with their main hoes. Not to mention the countless other pioneers who pimped so hard that they never knew a square bitch, yet still had kids.

I wondered how could these guys marry hoes and have kids with them without suffering for it if these were lines you should not cross. What was I missing in my understanding of how to walk a certain way without taking the wrong steps? It was the fact that making those hoes "a wife" was not the same as trying to turn her into a "housewife."

This is yet another example of how "understanding" something is more valuable than "remembering" something. Because a man can remember how to be a pimp and talk about it all day, repeating details, or he can understand how to put a mack hand down, and actually show you what moves to make.

A short lesson on the superiority of mack quality is as follows: Mack moves employ more means of reaching pimp-type goals while maintaining pimp-type principles. They follow the discipline of Ism while still steering a ho above and beyond limits of just selling sex. And this applies to both hustling and day-to-day life for the dedicated few who are serious enough about making sure this Game does what it's supposed to do.

That definition of mackin' actually embodies the answer to all the questions I had. These hoes were being happily handled by real macks, who could run their program and be known more for the pimp shit they do than whatever slick shit anybody could say out of his mouth.

The proof was their truth, and that proof came in the form of them knowing how to let a ho be a ho. They weren't afraid of the reality behind what those women were, and they understood how to accept one thing without letting emotions turn it into something else.

When you can do this, it's easy to keep it pimpin' instead of tryna put handcuffs on a good ho. Furthermore, you won't get worked up when she does some of the thing's hoes are known to do. Because you'll never expect anything less, your moves will be made with those kinds of possibilities in mind.

This kind of man takes the bitter with the sweet and never tries to make a ho into something she's not. Instead, they just roll with the punches like a master martial artist who has learned how to use the opponent's attack to their own advantage. Comparing them to the average pimp is like the difference between regular karate and the many styles of kung fu.

A successful pimp will become an eternal student of human nature. A successful student of any subject will learn from understanding and accepting the facts that apply to that subject they study. So, if you ever expect a ho to be anything else, you will not be very successful in this Game, because she can be a lot of things in addition to being a ho, but she'll never be anything instead of a ho.

Therefore, we can only increase her duties, abilities, personal possessions, and position in life when it comes down to the question of what to do with the hoes who choose us.

Let those hoes be hoes, no matter what else you may ever add to the list of parts she can play for you. And don't take her ho tendency personal, or you'll be cutting yourself short on opportunity because you'll end up doing things that will teach her to hold back on giving you her best, her last, and most profitable of all, her repeat performance.

You want her to respect your Ism for sure, but you also want her to know she can come home and make up for the mistakes all hoes make. She should never be so scared to fuck up that if she does you're sure to never see her again.

Pimpin' is more than just punishing prostitutes. It's about building special bonds with boss bitches based on gettin' money; not breaking a ho's spirit or holding hoes back.

In the end, you will win because your reputation as a gentleman who can let a ho be a ho will guarantee you this overall outcome.

You must learn to face the fact that hoes run off, hoes choose other pimps, hoes steal, hoes lie, and hoes can hurt your feelings. But hoes will also pay you, hoes will build you up, hoes will sacrifice their all to please you, and they accept things from you that a square bitch never would. So, if you pick the right hoes, and you're pimpin' the right way, the good will outweigh the bad. That's why you gotta let a ho be a ho, respect the Game, and accept it for what it is.

Let a ho be a ho without holding it against her, so her heart can have a home and she's not just another lost soul. Because hoes are people, too, and the good ones deserve a happy ending when that's what they've paid for.

So, if you're gonna pimp, then let a ho be a ho. Straight-the-fuck-up.

PURSE FIRST, ASS LAST

"Whether ya pimpin' is soft or hard, it shouldn't take long to break the broad."
— Too $hort

In the more advanced stages of pimpin', it can be said that closed legs get no bread. This is true. But it is also true that in the advanced stages of any Game being played, a successful player had better understand the rules and plays well enough to flip and twist that shit in more ways than just what's written in the rulebook.

How much can you bend it without breaking it? How much can you force it without taking it? How hard can you push without being too pushy? How hard or soft can you go while still not being a pussy?

The only way you can ever answer these questions truthfully is to provide the proof to see. So how you play it will always affect your life more than how you say it.

With this fact being established, let me point out the thing about a lot of rules. They can be observed and even followed in more than just one way. People live by rules, and a very large part of life is growth and development.

Guidelines are cool, but a mindset will take you further in life. So when I say to get the purse first and ass last, this should be your overall mindset. Because if it becomes a line you refuse to cross, then you may one day fall short at a time you need to be adjusting your Game to a particular set of circumstances that happen to call for you to get down different from how you normally do.

In the trenches, I once saw a self-proclaimed pimp play his hand straight out of the rulebook. He used to brag about how he was "Oh so serious" about his pimpin'. But by that time, I already knew that the people who do it like that are usually the ones who need the most work on improvement.

So, he used to scream "Purse first, ass last!" all the time because he had a bad bitch that he claimed he was not going to fuck until she paid him a certain amount of money. I used to hear him without really listening much because I figured the Game was new to this dude, or he wasn't as real as he said he was. Something about the way he was always bumpin' his gums on some shit that was elementary to me.

But we had mutual associates, so I was in position to observe this fool. I watched him, thinking one day he might blow his bitch and I could scoop her when he did.

Anyway, the story goes into ol' boy really being so down for his crown that he ain't givin' ol' girl no goodies. But at some point, she finally hit whatever goal he had set and he was happy, so he bought himself a nice car with the money and started givin' ol' girl the ding-dong.

I guess this could've worked out in his favor if this dude would've understood the principle behind what he did. But all he did was memorize a single step that he heard about somewhere along the way, so when it came down to what his next move should be, he was lost in the sauce.

So, he shows off his new car to everybody and starts to get down with his ho. But let's not forget that she was a bad bitch, therefore, once he started fuckin' her, he pretty much never did anything else.

As soon as she would get off work, he was in it. Then, throughout her time at work, he was pulling her off location to get a dose. First it was only a little bit, and then it was a lot. Then there started being days when he would let her get off early just so he could fuck the bitch himself.

It wasn't long before he started lettin' ol' girl not even go to work at all because they was caught up on some real punk shit. Cupcake pimpin' is what this dude started doing more and more, until it wasn't even pimpin' at all.

Soon ol' girl was pregnant, and since there were no real pimp principles in place at the foundation of his program, he never did get another ho. I'm sure by that point such a move was a serious no-no. And before too long he had to see the car she bought him to make up for the money she was no longer making.

The last time I saw this dude, he was in a fucked-up minivan on meth. Ol' girl had left him and he was on some soccer-mom-type shit with a couple of kids.

That's when I remembered what my O.G. potna Paul Tanner had told me in San Francisco about the dudes who got real hoes without bein' real pimps.

The guys out there who don't really do this will say all the sayings, but when it comes to runnin' the play for real, they fumble the ball.

Yeah, it is supposed to be purse first, ass last. But the ass can't ever replace the cash! Pimps do pimp shit to get paid, not to lay claim to any fame or just establish a recognizable name.

P.I.M.P. stands for Paper In My Pocket! Therefore, this should be the guideline about all else. Pay to play is the hustle. And this should be the cloud that covers every step you take, not just one avenue you walk down in a city full of streets. Because Ism dictates that you should never get from under this particular overcasting principle.

I was talkin' to my potna 'Twan from East Oakland the other day and he said something that sparked a memory. He's working with a super-bad little Asian bitch who calls herself his "foreign persuasion" because she's part Hispanic. But they get real money, though, and they got each other's back, so I respect their Game a lot.

Anyway, we was choppin' up some Game the other day and he told me that he don't even be wanting to fuck all the time like that. I was somewhat surprised because I happen to know that him and his folks are really into each other. Then, during the same conversation, he went on to tell me how lil mama says she feels the same way because all that emotional shit is out of place in our world since it gets in the way of business.

And right when I got ready to start asking some key questions, he hit me with a pimp twist that I know a square would never understand.

The first part of this twist was when he went from what he'd just said right into some off-handed remark about having sex with his folks. The second part of it came when he then spoke of another chick he fucks with but doesn't have any sex with at all. And yet that other chick just bought him a watch worth around forty bands.

That's when I had to silently salute my boy 'Twan because he had just showed me that he understood all the things I'd been tellin' him for years. As a matter of fact, he understood it so good that he helped me to understand it better, and this is the only reason I'm able to explain it now.

See, my nigga never said he *didn't* fuck like that. He said he don't be *wanting* to fuck like that. So when he does do it, he don't get all caught up and distracted wit' it. And he has an understanding with his folks about how it could hurt their hustle if they ever forget that the hustle is more important. So no matter how much they enjoy each other, the purse comes first because the ass don't replace the cash.

Then a memory came to me about my early beginnings. I'd just come up on my first real go-getter named Lanelle. I was so brand-new that I repeated a lot of the rules I'd heard about to myself all the time. So on our first night together, I was trying my best not to give in to my sexual desires with Lanelle.

But Lanelle was all the way the truth, and we had her mother's house to ourselves, so she wasn't trying to hear about how a nigga with a rock-hard dick wasn't tryna fuck, you feel me? She thought I was playin' with her and we ended up doin' the do anyway.

Her mother called in the middle of her ridin' me better than any other girl ever has, and she had to answer the phone. Once the call was done, she came back for more, but I held out after that.

She was exceptional in every way, so I never could refuse her for long, but because I knew I wasn't supposed to just fall for every opportunity, the pussy never became a distraction.

We were both still teenagers, so of course we fucked like a couple of rabbits. But our relationship wasn't built on having sex, though. She knew I was trying to stick to the script and get money, so that was how she played her way into the good times we had in bed.

I never had to ask Lanelle for anything. She was born and bred into the Game, so a lot of things either came natural to her, or she learned from her mama. Knowing I was on some Ism was enough to inspire her performance. Having it understood that I didn't wanna fuck like that motivated her to make sure I always felt like a player both in and out of bedroom situations. So no matter how much ass she gave me, our real priority was about the purse first.

Early each morning until late each night, she was ready and willing to get our money right. Anything she noticed that I liked, she made sure I got a lot of it. She cleaned my jewelry and pumped me up to buy even more. If there was a stray bitch within a ten-mile radius, Lanelle would sniff her out and bring her home to me. And once I taught her how to drive, she became my chauffer. Whatever it took to increase my level, she was about that to the fullest.

So keep the purse first on your personal list of what is important to you, and you'll keep it pimpin' no matter what else you do. The ass comes last in this same way, which is the order of importance. That way, even if fuckin' a bitch is the first things you do, you won't lose sight of what the business is. Because if the pussy moves you more than the money does, you're entertaining the wrong hustle.

As a pimp, you play the role of the manager to all things that matter. You manage the time, you manage the money, you manage the ho, etc. And a large part of successful management is the application or moderation. Everybody gets a break as long as the breaks don't outweigh the work. This is the principle of moderation; you don't do too much.

So when you manage yourself and all your extra activities, you should be making sure you're not getting high on your own supply more than you're getting paid from it.

In this new-wave era of whatever it is these squares are tryna do in the place of Ism, you got clowns handcuffing these hoes out there. They hold her hostage and hide her from some real pimpin' in hopes that she will one day decide she's in love with them. These same clowns run around with the bitch never far from them, entertaining people's eyes with the view, but never putting that ho to work like he 'posed to do. Then they claim it's big pimpin' when they've never even sent that bitch to the corner store.

This kind of punk-ass substitute for real shit is a lot more common than people think. Giving the Game a black eye behind closed doors seems to be what's in style now. But if a pimp goes for the purse first, ass last philosophy, it would be impossible to fall into such a false representation of what he's supposed to be.

When a man lets himself be distracted so extremely from his purpose like this, it's probably for one of two reasons. Either he has a smart ho who has turned him into the only trick she needs with a bunch of promises about what she's going to do and how good they're going to be, or he has a ho who's as dumb as he is that he doesn't have a clue about what a real one is supposed to do. Each one of these possible reasons are examples of the blind leading the blind.

A pimp is supposed to somehow separate himself from the herd of horny men out there who only wish to have a ho satisfy their sexual needs. He's not supposed to fall down in the mud with the bitch and make his home there.

The only thing you should ever do more than you send your provider to get that money is talk to her, listen to her, learn her inside and out, and let her learn to understand your vision. That way you know how to teach her what you see she needs to know. And you'll learn how to say things in the ways she will listen to the most. But anything beyond that should fall into an everlasting chase of the chalupa! For those who don't know, that means you and that ho should be scrapin' for the scratch, scratchin' for the scrilla, and chompin' at the chance to check your cheese. In other words, get that money, man! Because anything less is not pimpin'.

IT AIN'T THE BEAUTY, IT'S THE DUTY

"The best looker don't make the best hooker."
– Old Pimp Proverb

A lot of niggas out there come into the Game thinkin' that you 'posed to only pimp on "bad bitches" if you doin' it for real. But the best lookers don't always make the best hookers. So what does it mean to be a "bad bitch"?

A well-known madam once said she would rather have a team full of sevens who liked to have fun than a team full of tens who felt like somebody owed them something. And she was one of the biggest in Hollywood history.

Experience has brought me to the same conclusion. After years of observing countless players operate, and also runnin' my own plays under all kinds of conditions and circumstances I can honestly say that the percentage of positive results is higher among those whose beauty was not so obvious to see at first sight.

So, I would start this segment of the discussion by saying this: A bad bitch and a pretty bitch ain't always the same thing.

You cannot look at the women you see on TV or in magazines and think that's the definition of a bad bitch. Even though those are some bad bitches, your eyes are playing a trick on your mind when you think you're understanding what makes them "bad."

Show business and the media is based mostly on visual entertainment. So, most of the women you see in that business will be able to appeal to the visual sense because that's their job. They are in the business of looking good, so they are handlin' their business by being attractive to your eyes. And the more these girls get paid for lookin' good, the more they will invest in what will enhance their appearance.

But if you find a random chick at a club or walking down the street whose beauty compares to what you see on TV, you might be disappointed in the end if you expect everything in life to fall into place just because she looks good.

First of all, she might be bat-shit crazy. Second, she might be the laziest person you ever met in your life. And if either one of these is the case, she can't be called a bad bitch in a pimp's opinion. Maybe more like a bad experience, or even a bad decision, but not a bad bitch in terms of what you should be lookin' for. Because a bad bitch is a bitch who handles her business. That's the number one non-negotiable requirement for any consideration in a pimp's judgement. If she don't handle your business, then she's the worst thing ever – the most unattractive thing you've ever seen. Period!

So, if you're not lookin' at a media star, then it takes a lot more than just being pretty to qualify as a bad bitch. The result is what matters most in this Game, and it can be very easy for your pimpin' to become trickin' if you tell yourself that you'll only function with the prettiest girls you can find.

I prefer the most productive girls I can find above and beyond all else. And then they must be willing to cooperate with my Ism, or we're not going to be any good to each other at all. So that's why it can be said that a real P will put a wig on a pig or a girdle on a turtle when it comes down to chasin' his cheese. Because how she looks has nothin' to do with what makes her beautiful, in my eyes.

One man's trash is another man's treasure in the high-performance world of gold diggers and go-getters. And smart people don't judge books by their covers. So, anyone who thinks they can look at a woman and properly judge if she's a bad bitch or not has a lot of learning let to do.

I remember when this lesson first really hit home for me. It was on a trip down to the Los Angeles area one summer with my buddy T-Roy from East Oakland. He had a tall, slim, curvaceous brown-skinned go-getter who knew how to hustle and had already proven she could get money anywhere he put her to work. I had a cute lil chubby chick I'd just turned out who was nowhere near as experienced or eye-catching as T-Roy's work was, but I knew she was down for me, and that's what I had on my team at the moment.

So, we get out to Anaheim and the track is off the hook with hoes everywhere. I mean, all up and down the main boulevard, every hotel and motel was poppin' with prostitution in at least ten different rooms. You would have thought this hustle wasn't even against the law with the way it was going down everywhere we looked.

Some might think that this would be a pimp's paradise, and that could be true, but competition is what came to my mind, because there were some "bad" bitches walking around out there lookin' good in high heels and sexy clothes. And my lil folks was so flat-footed that it was downright cruelty to put her out there in high heels for hours at a time. I'd tried it already, and her little feet was so torn up, she could barely walk! So in order for the bitch to put in any time, I had to put her in sandals, and even that was hard on her feet. This would put her at a disadvantage next to a wide selection of hoes lookin' like sexy video vixens in high heels.

But I didn't need any advantage as much as I needed a ho willing to go. So, at the end of the day, in the face of all my fears, I decided I had no choice other than to just pimp past my doubts.

The only move to make was to get right to work, because it was really jumpin' that hard when we arrived. This removed any room for anything more than a quick pep talk and some promises of delivering something to eat. It was off to the races after that.

Now when I say it was really jumpin', I mean these hoes wasn't even makin' it out of the parking lot before they caught another date to take back to their rooms. So, the situation was serious about how hard those girls were trying to make sure they caught the eye of every trick in sight. And I saw a lot of potential customers pulling over for one girl, only to change his mind and choose another once he got out of his car.

None of the pimps wanted to disturb the traffic in any way, so everybody on some Ism remained in their cars parked in the cuts where they could watch the show. But it was so crowded that seeing everything was impossible, so I had no view of my own situation from where I was parked. However, I saw enough of what other girls were doing to know it was poppin', and to keep up with how it was poppin'.

There was one girl in particular who I noticed that stood out to me because of how many tricks she turned away. She was super attractive in a G-string bikini with some kind of see-through material tied around her waist like a skirt. Ass all over the place, in high heels with the sexy walk to set it all off, I couldn't keep myself from watching once I saw her. But that's what made it obvious to me after a couple of hours that she was bullshitting more than I would want anyone representing me to try and get away with. And still she was done long before the money flow slowed down enough to justify calling it quits.

That next morning, me and my buddy were both excited to say that our bankroll came in to be around twelve hundred dollars. But privately I was surprised that my little folks had kept up with his, because he had a vet and mine was a new-booty.

I was further surprised by my new-booty when she kept those same kind of numbers up night after night, and T-Roy's work never managed to beat her by more than a hundred dollars. Then one day I met a dude whose name I don't remember even though I'll never forget him because of the lesson I learned by running into him.

He was at the 7-Eleven down the street from my hotel, and I'd seen his Cadillac around enough to know he was on the same hype I was on. So I hit him up about where to find some weed and we got to talking. Somewhere in the conversation his willingness to sell his car came up, but I was happy with the BMW I was driving so I passed on the offer.

His weed stash was back at his room, so he had me follow him there to buy a couple bags from him. He said he would match a blunt with me before we got back to our traps, and that sounded good since I was the only person in my circle who smoked weed. So off we went on our mission to be entertained by Mary Jane.

When we got back to the hotel, I hopped into the Caddy with ol' boy while he was on the phone with his peoples giving the order for the trees. Once he had that done, he explained that his bitch was gonna bring it out to us, so we settled into choppin' Game while we waited.

In the way that pimps do whoever they first meet, we shot the shit back and forth to indirectly compare our level of Game with one another. That's when I really got a chance to verify that he was, in fact, authentic with a so-so piece of work at the moment. I had to respect that he didn't try to sauce it up, either. He just laughingly made reference to the fact that she wasn't the worst but was far from the best, and how he couldn't wait until the Game God blessed him with the next.

"Oh, here come that ol' short-change-ass bitch now," he said offhandedly as his folks made her way to the car.

Always curious about a ho, I looked to see which one of the bitches I'd been seein' out there hustlin' was his. And wouldn't you know, it was that same ho who stood out to me that first night! She was just as fine as ever, but I remembered what her own man had just said about her, as well as how I myself had seen her hustle. And all my eyes showed me right then was the fact that the best lookers really don't automatically make the best hookers.

That bitch looked like a model for real, and yet she wasn't even half the woman my folks was. As time went by, this proved to be true on more than just a ho level, too, because the particular girl I was working with at the time went on to explore at least two other hustles on top of eventually going square to work for the county in San Francisco. Through community college and all, she shined. And everywhere I put her down on that trip, she rocked that shit like a vet.

I'm not saying that good looking women are all bad. I'm saying that if you pick them just based on if they're pretty or not, you'll probably get more bad ones than good ones; and not the kind of "bad" you're lookin for, either. Your ho money will more than likely come second or even third to your ho troubles.

Another thing I've noticed is that the law is a lot more enthusiastic about putting pimps in jail for extreme amounts of time than they were back in the day. The main tool they use to achieve this goal is to charge the pimp with having an underage girl. For this reason, it's very important that you keep it above legal age. But I will also warn you that the quickest way to get tricked into overlooking the safety measures that should protect you from this trap is to let yourself be moved by very pretty faces.

As I said before, a bad bitch is one who handles business. So an ability to handle business is the most important quality I think a pimp should look for. Then you're going to need her to be about your business, which is not always the case among people you meet in this Game. There are more important requirements any woman should meet in order for you to team up with her, and they're so valuable that once you find them you would be a fool to pass on them just because the girl who has them is not the prettiest one in the room.

In my opinion, a ho would sound like a real idiot is she came to me talking about how she's refusing money because the tricks aren't cute enough. So, what does that say about a pimp who only wants to get paid from pretty hoes?

I would suggest you consider a goose that gives you golden eggs before you take that pretty chicken who's only giving you the average omlette. And I would call anyone a complete fool if he picked a beautiful swan that gave up nothing but rotten eggs, or even worse, no eggs at all.

This doesn't only apply to the appearance of the hoes you choose to work with. It stands just as strong in reference to your working situation as well. So don't let yourself be out there chasing only the pretty dreams, because you will soon learn that it's the ugly reality that pays off on a more steady, dependable basis.

If you plan on gettin' money every single day like you're supposed to do, then you will need to lose those ideas of only dealing with rich, easy tricks that spend big money each and every time. That kind of fantasy might work for a weekend warrior, but not a real hustler who is trying to really see some money out of this hustle.

What's real is this: You will stack the most when you collect a lot of the least. That's why Little Caesar's Pizza had a lot of those other pizza joints with their backs against the wall. Because people were buying more of those five-dollar pizzas than they were the more expensive ones from other places.

One time I met a little player from Atlanta who had a cute little Asian chick out of California. They had just gotten to Virginia and were doing their thing while I happened to be in town working a couple of girls I had at the time.

In that part of the country, the economy is good because a lot of people have government-related jobs. This is true, but it's only the first part of a multi-layered truth about why the money out there is so sweet.

So, the youngster is out there expecting to get it good with his exotic piece of work, but everywhere he goes only gives him chump change compared to what I was getting at the same spots.

The folks was a slick lil dude from that Zone 6 area in East Atlanta, so it didn't take him long to see that I was eating better than he was.

"My nigga, how the fuck is my bitch out here barely doin' better than we do back home, while you out here buyin' 'Benzes and shit?" he asked me one day while we chopped up the Game while our hoes were working.

I must admit that I'm not the all-seeing eye of pimpin', so I didn't know the answer to his question. And I was honest enough to tell him this truth. But at the same time, I was actually wondering the same thing myself, so his question opened the door to a deeper discussion. Together we would discover the answer.

As we talked, though, I got more confused, because he was not very far from me with his work ethic. His ho wasn't lazy, and she didn't turn down money. Or did she?

The rest of the reason why money is so sweet back east is because everybody except a pimp (and in some cases pimps, too) can be a trick. They just buy pussy a lot more freely and politely out there. So a real provider has far more chances to get paid than she does in the west. This is because in the west you don't really want her to date Black guys who usually think they can do more than they should for one reason or another. But the further east you go, the more it seems to be OK for your team to safely date Black guys, as long as they stick to being about business.

So when we got around to his folks not turning down no money, I ran down all the little ways that I had seen my hoes make short money tricks add up to big money traps. And he told me his ho was up on all of that, but then he complained about how he noticed that most of the calls he got for those deals were Black dudes.

"That's good for you, though, bruh. You want the niggas in and out instead of spendin' all day tryin' some extra shit," I said, thinking he knew it was cool.

It was then that we recognized the difference between my Ism and his. He had a Southern California ho who knew the same rule that Northern California had taught me about how Black guys can turn out to be pimps in disguise, or otherwise up to no good, so are best to be ignored. But I knew that the rule faded as I left the west coast, so I enjoyed days where almost all of my money came from fifteen-minute short stays and half-hour specials that the Black guys ate up like candy, while my poor little pimpin' potna was unable to get his ho to adjust. She was turnin' down what would've added up to more money than she'd ever gotten before on some regular everyday ho work.

I didn't want the youngsta to feel like I was tryna steer him into a wreck, so I didn't press the issue about the mistake he was making. A few words of enlightenment was all I offered him before I left it alone. But it was clear to see that his income suffered as a result of only wanting the money that came in an attractive package.

I remember another time, further back, when I was starting over from scratch with only one turnout on my team. She was a real pretty red bone with blue-green eyes who got a lot of attention everywhere we went, so I didn't want to just immediately throw her to the wolves in Oakland or San Francisco, and that's why I decided to work her in a small town across the Richmond bridge called San Rafael.

Oakland would have been the right place to go if getting seen by all the players is what I wanted. San Francisco would've been the fast city experience most girls come to the Bay Area looking for. But for sure both places would've satisfied the look more than the result, because ol' girl would've spent more time dodging pimps than getting money.

Since I was trying to bounce back from nothing, I needed my situation to focus more on coming up while she also learned how to do her job. I had no time or patience for the political parts of pimpin', so I socialized very little and did my own thing.

San Rafael will bring a ho nothing but the migrant workers who will only spend small amounts of money, but she will get a steady flow of customers every single night, and for the most part she'll be safe. So even though it's not glamorous, you'll for sure get paid.

After a few weeks of breaking her in out there, I bought a car and hit the road with her. We went up to Portland, Oregon and Seattle, Washington. The track in Seattle was pretty fast-paced, and she did just fine.

But the truth was that she did better in San Rafael than she did anywhere else. So even though it was boring out there after a while, we stuck to the steady, for-sure money instead of jumping around playing hit and miss like everybody else was doing. And we came up just as good or better as my pimp potnas who were going to Oakland or San Francisco every night. Because how it paid off was more important than what we saw when we looked at it.

The duty of your situation is the same as the duty of your ho, which is to bring the most money with the least problems. Any other consideration is based on bullshit, and this includes appearances.

THEY'RE PROMISED TO PAY, NOT TO STAY

"Play every day like it's your last day."
– Old Pimp Proverb

I read a book once when I was young about a pimp from Baltimore named Junius. He was unique in the world of pimps and hoes in a lot of ways, and I have a very high regard for every book he was ever in.

I remember one of the stories had a part in which he had his eye on a ho he was about to knock, and he was plottin' on the move he was gonna make. As he looked at her, he told himself that he saw eight years in her. He counted eight wardrobe changes, eight Cadillac changes, and eight sets of jewelry in his future from her.

Even though I can honestly say that I learned quite a few very useful things from that story and all the rest that featured that character, the eight-year plan was and is pure fantasy, because the book has never been written that can give anybody the Game on how to be sure of what a ho will do next. Hoes are promised to pay, not to stay. So, when you play from day to day, play every day as if it is the last day.

This is not to say that you should treat her as if she's about to leave. And this does not mean that all hoes have an evil plan to eventually leave you high and dry. What I'm sayin' is that we live in a very cynical world. And anyone who has an aim to properly play this Game should know that

141

the only thing you can control for sure is yourself. It's not about trying to beat your brain up or bully her brain into being what you want it to be. It's about making the most out of all things that do go your way, because you never know when things will change.

You may have the most loyal team in the whole world, or you might be working with a situation that will last a lifetime. But if you take it for granted, you stand a chance of killing every bit of whatever good might exist in your mix.

There is a very thin line between love and hate when you're in the business of making people think that you're happy. You cannot turn an intentionally unhappy person into a happy one. So it all starts with what they think about you.

Being in the business of relating to people puts our thoughts and feelings on the frontline, though, because there will be the constant exposure to all the many things that can have an effect on us. So from day to day, there's no way to know what will come your way. Therefore, you never know as a pimp the whole hundred percent of what to expect from your ho. As a major part of this Game, she too can always fall under the influence of whatever hand you may happen to be dealt.

My greatest heartbreaks in life have all come to me without any warning at all. And usually, they even occurred on the tail end of something else happening that led me to believe that whatever was done was the last thing they would ever do.

But as I got older and time moved me further away from the initial sting of the bite, I can look back and see that there was probably more to each situation than just what hurt my feelings. There are always things that will happen in life; things beyond our control that we must respond to. So the truth is that those girls may not even have known themselves that they were going to do what they did.

I myself have had my back against the wall in ways that forced moves on my part that were no so sweet. So even a super solid member of your team may unexpectedly encounter a situation that changes the Game. This is why the saying goes, "Don't hate the player, hate the Game."

These hoes are on the playing field just like you, so they count as players, too. That's why you have to be on top of your shit if you don't want the shit to fall on top of you.

This is where your application of Socialism comes into play. Because to a certain extent, you can benefit from making sure you look out for your folks making sure they get the things they want and need is the most important thing you can do. But your job is to do this in a way that won't break the bank.

In the process of doing this, you will be managing your situation, which includes managing your money. So in the end, you give ol' girl a real reason to stick around, but you also give yourself something left over if she ever decides to go on about her business.

If a dude loses his girl to the next man and ends up trying to get all gangster with his response instead of accepting the news like a real P, you can bet it's probably because she's leaving his ass broke. That's when those kinds of dudes start coming up with all kinds of imaginary things they feel like the girl "owes" them for. This is a sad position to be in, and it should be an embarrassment to a real P, because it shows a man who is so damn down and out, that he's still depending on a ho that doesn't even want him anymore. That's like half a step away from aggressive panhandling.

So, take pride in your craft and the image you are supposed to maintain as a pimp. Stack your money before you spend any of it. That way you can afford to do bigger things. And most importantly, you won't be stuck on empty if you wake up one day with the Game deciding that it's time to separate you from your provider.

Then be realistic enough to always know that anything might happen when you're dealing with your ho. Curiosity kills the cat more often than a lot of people want to admit. And this leads mankind in general astray at the most unexpected rate of frequency.

The Prince of Arabia could pop up one day and offer your provider a cakewalk of an existence as his mistress. Anything she wants, she gets, just to fuck him once a week, as long as she leaves you and stops being a ho. Sure, you might get that bitch back after she realizes he's into some strange shit she don't wanna do. But until then, chances are that you're probably going to lose that ho.

Now, the most relevant fact to be found in that example is that it won't take the Prince of Arabia to put you in that position. A ho can come across a big-money trick anywhere in the world. And since she is a professional at meeting men, it doesn't even have to be a trick. The point is that she just might pick something that looks better one day.

Another thing that can work against you is the fact that some people hold grudges. And since pimpin' is not always the friendliest thing to do, there's never any telling when you may bust a move that will not be forgiven. So if you're the type that likes to go hard or talk bad, please believe that any day she might decide to walk away.

I even remember growing up hearing horror stories of the pimp whose ho's were oh-so-good that his jewelry Game was legendary. But one day he either went to sleep of they put something in his drink, and when he woke up, those bitches had taken everything, never to be seen or heard from again.

There were other real-life stories about real good pimps that many looked up to who had real good hoes. One of those pimps in particular had a ho named Nikki that I'm sure any P out there would've wanted on his team. But the more I learned about her, the more I came to know that she left her folks so many times that I'm convinced that a part of their program must have included blowing up as an established ingredient to the recipe of real success. Because in spite of her coming and going, she had that man rich in every way.

As a rule, in this Game, you must take the bitter with the sweet. Many of the hoes that gave me the most also hurt me the most until I was seasoned enough to stop attaching my feelings to the things they did wrong. That's just a given in the Game we play, and nobody is going to change it. You want the rose? Be ready for the thorns that come with it.

Once I got that understanding, it was nothing for a ho to leave me. I had sense enough to stack the money up, and my absence of anger even kept the door open for most of those hoes to come back. In those situations, they usually don't mind making up for what they did, so with a little bit of sauce poured onto a lore more Game, I managed to come up even more at the end of the day.

The only person who won't expect his ho to ever run off is an impostor who is really a ho's boyfriend and not really pimpin' at all. People like that usually thrive on promises, and were probably waiting on her to make good on one when she decided she'd rather get gone than keep it solid.

It's a law of nature that weakness is never, ever rewarded at all. When another life form comes across a weakness, instinct will lead it to exploit that weakness in some way. This is set in our DNA, so we cannot change it. Therefore, when that ho spots a weakness of believing bullshit, or going for the okey-doke in her folks, you better believe she's going to bite him at some point. So don't ever wait until later when it's time to get down with your paperchase. Never make excuses, and for sure don't accept any excuse. Pimp past all of that and get paid because that ho might not be there at the designated time, then you'll be left high and dry while she's off on another adventure.

I've seen hoes go home with a dude under the false pretense of choosin' up, just so he can take her shopping. Once that was out of the way, she was gone the first chance she got to get away with what ol' boy bought her.

In another situation, there have been hoes who chose one pimp just to get away from the one they were with. And as soon as the new P served the news to the old one, that bitch was gone, on about her business, free from the worry of that first pimp's punishment.

The common connection that these situations share is the fact that these dudes were victimized by the beast of expectation. They expected those hoes to come correct when they should've required it up front before anything else was able to take place.

If the ho won't get paid by fuckin' a trick for free, then how can she expect a free ride out of a real P? A real one would never even ask you to go for anything like that because she knows that this is a money Game.

I knocked a ho once on a fluke in Oakland on some late-night-hype-type shit. I had heard about her somewhere along the way but never met her. So, when I saw her from a distance, I called her by her name just to see if she would come to me. The timing must've been perfect because everything went my way, and I knew I really had her because of how I ran my play.

But we had one hiccup that could've put me in a real trick bag if I made the wrong move in response to it. She had just gotten started at her work, so the only money she had so far was eighty bucks, and some square was in the area thinking she was out there for him. For this reason, I couldn't just leave her out there to keep working.

So off we went with the chump change in my pocket and the ho in my car. But when she apologized for how small her contribution was, I let her know it was OK because she could add to it. Then without any hesitation, I hit the Bay Bridge and put her down on the San Francisco track before doing anything else.

Within a few more hours, she got me another five hundred dollars, and our ship sailed off in the right direction. I was juiced to have this blonde haired, blue eyed snow bunny whose name was well-known in the Game, because I just knew I was about to come up on a whole lot of money and braggin' rights.

The next night she got me eight hundred more dollars and we developed a plan to hit the road.

All we did was talk when she wasn't working. I hit it a few times, and we got drunk, but mostly we chopped it up and really got into vibing with each other. And it was during these talks that I discovered ol' girl was on parole, running from a violation. This was back when violations were up to a year at a time.

The next night she got snatched up on a warrant and I never saw her again. I had no way to find her because the only name I knew her by was "Snow," and she'd given an alias when she went to prison, so her first name wasn't going to help me. So that was a done deal; even though if it was up to her she would've stayed, the Game took her away.

At the end of it all, the only thing I had was the ability to be glad that she left me with some money. Not so much for the sake of the money itself, but the fact that I knew I could've easily wasted those two days. Because this ho and the connection we had was so official, there was no doubt at all about how good the situation was about to be.

But if I would not have bet on that instead of sending her to work, I would've been left with nothing at all except a broken dream. This could have crossed over into some broken pockets, too, if I would've been the type to financially fertilize a possible payoff.

The proof is the truth, and a promise ain't the proof. So when you see potential, make it prove what it's worth. Don't just promise yourself it will pay off, because if you do, that promise will take the place of that payoff. And the payoff itself will never come to a person who is willing to settle for substitutes.

Don't ever let yourself feel like you know for sure if your ho is still going to be there the next day. The only thing you can be sure about is that if you stick to the script, she will pay you until she's gone. And if she never leaves, then maybe you've been blessed. Just hope that she's a good one and give her whatever good she deserves, because if you did it right, she paid your price.

CHECKIN' AIN'T CHEATIN'

"Stay on top of your game!"
– Bishop Don Juan

Checkin' ain't cheatin' when it comes to finding out if a situation will work out for you or not. The Game we play requires us to shoot our shot if we want to be sure we can score in the arena of slick-talkin' competition.

There have been a lot of times when I've looked back at the past and saw things that made me wish I would've done more to explore what was possible with the opportunities I encountered along the way.

You will never know if a girl will go for you unless you check. And you will never know if a ho will contribute to your cause unless you check to see. So, as a professional pimp, you're never wrong for checking out a chance to do what you do.

Sometimes the female you're talking to is unsure about you and won't come right out to say she's not ready to pay your pimpin'. Other times, she may not even know she has it in her to go your way unless you bring it up to her.

But there's a very fine line between discovery and disrespect, so at the same time that you're being bold, you must also remain mindful of how you're being received. That's where finesse comes into play. Because if you gotta let a ho be a ho, then you gotta let a square be a square if that's her choice. So, we don't just run our play blindly without knowing if we're talking to the right people. We keep our eyes open, and when we see an opportunity to do our thang, we pimp.

A pimp in an opportunist who employs a method of making things happen that is very similar to gold mining. He grabs up the dirt and the rocks right along with the gold he's going for, then he sifts it all around in an effort to separate what he wants from the rest of what surrounds it.

A place with a lot of women to choose from is just like a gold mine to a real P. And the only way he can find out which of those women are what he wants is to check and see. He has to talk to them, watch them, and listen to what they say.

The questions he should be asking himself are: Who is with the idea of choosin' up? Who would go good with the program you have in place? Which one is sincere? Etc. Or, if a rival pimp shows up with some hoes: Are they all happy? Is ol' boy's Game tight? Would any of them ever choose you? Or, if it's just a single girl you happen to meet: Would she ever consider bein' a ho? What ways could she contribute to your cause?

To answer these kinds of questions, you have to dig into the kinds of discussion that will expose the good and the bad. The dynamics of this Game are so movable that you'll never know what might be possible. So, it would be stupid to not know what you can do in a Game where just about anything can happen. That's why checkin' ain't cheatin', because cheati is to break the rules of the Game, but checkin' is a major part of the Game you're in. Therefore, a smart pimp will always find a way to poke at seeing what he can do.

The older I get, the more I have to look back on and learn from. Even though I've forgotten more about the Game than most people will ever know, the one thing that never slips past my recognition is the chances I missed because of not doing more to turn things into what they could've been.

This applies to what I could've achieved with myself as well as other people, in both the pimp Game and regular life. You'll never know until you try.

So, checkin' ain't cheatin' in a life that needs you to make things happen if you don't want the Game to pass you by. Because the only way your Ism is going to grow is by you stretching it beyond its original size. This means you must do bigger, better, and bolder things to progressively benefit yourself more and more.

When that bad bitch crosses your path, you better take a crack at the ho. And when you hear how it's poppin' outta town somewhere far away, you'd better go see what it's all about.

If that watch costs ten bands, you need to see if you can save a few stacks before you hand over the full price. And when you go to buy that car you've been savin' up for, my nigga, why not at least look around to see how close you might be to buying the very best you can afford?

Because checkin' ain't cheatin'.

You'll get more and have more when you reach for more. You'll be more and see more when you try more, so when we check to see how much more is possible, we open the doors for whatever goodness the Game holds in store for us.

Let's go for it. Let's peek and peck at it. Let's always be checkin' for it. Because these forms of diggin' are the only ways we will know what treasure lies beneath the surface of what we see. And we have nothing to lose when this is our job anyway.

Almost every bitch that ever turned out for me managed to surprise me when she said "Yes." And what surprised me even more was the number of times I ran into those who ended up telling me that they had already tried the ho Game before ever meeting me. If I had never checked to see, I would've never known it was cool to pimp. But in shooting my shot, regardless of any doubts, I made a lot of things happen for me and those who chose my pimpin'.

I'm sure that the Game doesn't bless those who give it a black eye. So, my checkin' must have been a big part of what I was supposed to do. Because one thing I know for sure is that you miss a hundred percent of the shots you don't take. That's why you should always take your shot when you see it might be open for you.

The hustle and struggle demand that we shoot our shot! Anything less is characteristic of the audience, not the player. And you're not in the Game to watch the plays go by, right?

Remember that...

Most of your plays won't walk up to you with a sign strapped on that says they want to pay your pimpin'. Some might not even show their potential at first. And many of your opportunities won't be planning to benefit you when you first meet them, so if you don't check, chances are you'll never know what can be your next best move.

She can be right in your face just waiting to see how you're going to come at her about what she already knows she wants to give you. But if you never take a crack at her, she'll never be yours at all.

I've known many women throughout my life who knew they were worthwhile or extremely beautiful, but they would never on their own speak to a man if he didn't approach them first. I've also known many who were not sure they'd be wanted, and would never risk rejection by trying to get at a man who didn't get at them first. And a very high percentage of women are a combination of both types I just mentioned.

So, it's almost a guarantee that if you know you've got anything attractive about yourself, you've got action at a large majority of the women you meet. But more than half of them will never let you know it if you don't show any interest. And only a fool would think that every woman on earth wants him. That means you've got a lot of checkin' to do if you're going to find out which ones can go for you.

There are a chosen few who will be placed in your path to take your Game to the next step on your journey. The next place you hear about might be where you're meant to finally do it big. The owner of that car that catches your eye just might be sick of it, or struggling through a financial crisis that calls for him to sell it. What all these things share in common with each other is the fact that they need you to check them out before they give you the goodness they possess.

So, I suggest you get to checkin' or you might just cheat yourself out of everything you're supposed to have, be, or see.

In a pimp's Game, checkin' ain't cheatin'. This will forever be an undeniable fact.

IGNORE THE HATERS!

"Feel free to hate on me!"
– Kat Williams

I'm a professional rule breaker, a chronic risk taker, and a man who does the disrespectful while meaning no disrespect. I don't expect all the people who know me to love everything about the kind of man that I am, and I know that they won't. But I'm a real player, too, so if the opposite of love is hate, then those people are technically player haters for not loving me. Because if they know me, they must admit I've done nothing to them, so their negative feelings are unjustified.

But I also know that it's a serious waste of time and energy to worry about those people. So, beyond the point of trying to avoid them, I know it's best to pay them no attention.

Everybody in the jungle has to eat, and different breeds will feed on different forms of food. What satisfies your daily survival might be more than someone else can handle, so they have to settle for surviving on what's available to them. Unfortunately, that just might be the crumb-craving existence of hating on you while you get long bread and bypass short cake in your life.

A lot of people in this hip-hop generation put too much energy into acknowledging haters. They tease them, threaten them, and even go so far as to allow ongoing beef to exist with them.

I can agree wholeheartedly with not being no punk. You should always let enemies know what's up if they try to play you wrong. But that doesn't mean I agree with stepping away from a winning position in life to become a crash dummy just because a clown decides they don't like you. Because if you're in your lane, you shouldn't even notice their lane, right?

If you don't stand for something, you'll fall for anything. So if someone is really on some player shit, I don't see how they should ever be recognizing someone else who's not doing what they do. Because as a pimp, they should be pimping past all that non-related activity.

I once met a very ambitious little dude in Las Vegas who was real new to the Game. He tried hard enough to make it impossible for him to not come up on a little action here and there. So even though he didn't keep 'em, and never got any real money out of 'em, he did snag a few hoes.

I'm sure that in time, experience would've improved his results if he would've only been more about making pimp moves than he was about running head first into conflicts with people. But I found myself staying at a safe distance from him more than I felt any urge to lace him with Game, because his focus never failed to fall into how sure he was that everybody's eyes were on us, and how hard they thought they was, etc., etc.

The few times I did talk to him, I tried to guide our conversation to more worthwhile subjects, but you can't make nobody get it who don't really want it. And this little dude was more into justifying mistakes than correcting them.

So, one day, he knocks a cute little young ho from somebody, and he decides that it's more important to get into some smoke with the dude than it was to get to pimpin' on ol' girl. They argued over the phone, talked a lot of tough guy shit, and kept it all ugly.

Then, to go from bad to worse, the little crash artist sees the guy in traffic, and instead of driving on by, he pulls over to bounce out on ol' boy. The dude clutched on the youngster when he ran up on him, and the youngster whipped out his hammer to bang ol' boy three times

This story ends with the youngster going to prison on a four-year beef after fighting to avoid attempted murder charges. On top of that, he lost the ho that all the trouble was over, and also lost the ho he already had, along with his car, clothes, jewelry, etc.

So, in the end, the hater won.

Now, the everlasting question is: Why on earth would anybody go from winning to losing on purpose like that? And then blame their loss on the sucka for snitchin' on him, when he was the one who made it possible?

When that youngster got that man for that ho, he had the victory. Of course, the loser of that play might be upset, but how does that affect the winner? That youngster had nothing to be mad about. Period. So, when he took that fall, it was actually a jump on his part. He chose to fumble the ball instead of run it into a touchdown.

That's a perfect example of one way a hater can be sink your ship if you pay them too much attention, but it's not, by a long shot, the only example. You could get lost in all the ways a hater can mix you up, because there's just that many.

Therefore, the only sensible way to deal with a hater is to not deal with a hater. Hating is what they do. So just let them hate, and don't allow it to get the best of you.

Another part of this lesson is to remember that haters don't always start off as haters. Sometimes they begin as people in your circle who you've cut loose for some reason. This is why it's so important to be careful who you associate yourself with. Because it's hard to know exactly who will come back to bite you, and all money ain't good money when some money is just bait on a trap to get you caught up.

Real players play to win, and I'd rather lose a possibility than gain a problem. So even though it's said that a scared man can't win, I say it's stupid not to keep enough fear in you to make you careful.

The overall fact of the matter is that you should be going the opposite way whenever you come across someone who is not wishing wellness upon the things that you do. Focus on your craft and keep it pimpin'.

There are times when a good thing can go bad on you in ways you're not prepared for. I remember when I first learned this lesson, it was kind of late in the Game for me. I was getting good results, so I thought I was beyond the reach of a bad situation. That's how it caught me off-guard.

In one of my less-than-perfect moments, I made a ho mad and allowed my pride to keep me from making up for my mistake. She was such a real individual, I never expected her to switch up on me. So, when she did switch gears on how she got down, my disappointment only left room for dismissal. The details to that whole situation might make up a whole chapter on their own, but for now, I bring it up to point out how one thing can turn into another.

Anyway, the particular person we're discussing became one of my haters after she was cancelled out of my life. But her hating couldn't hurt me because I knew I had to separate her from the team I had working in the Midwest. So, when she saw that there was no way to pollute my program, she settled for making a real nuisance of herself.

Now here is how a hater can poison your pimpin' from a distance if you pay them too much attention. First off, the spirit of a spiteful intention becomes contagious. So, when I caught the bug from her, it manifested itself in the form of answering her calls just to let my continued success be known.

After a while of showing off, I was privately proud of how well I did in spite of her wishing bad on me. So proud, that it wasn't enough to just throw it in her face. I developed the need to speak on it to my social circle, too, and this included the hoes I had at

the time.

The ineffective efforts to create drama became so frequent that ol' girl became the example I brought up whenever I spoke on being hated. But what slipped past my defense was the

fact that I was now talking about this person far more than I should have, so indirectly she still managed to put herself into my business, and I was the one who helped make it happen.

I caught on to the damage being done when I was smoking a blunt with one of my hoes and she offhandedly said to me, "I Hope you know you got my wifey thinkin' you was in love with that bitch you keep talkin' 'bout. She swears it's the only reason you would ever bring her up so much."

That's when my weed-stimulated mind clicked into the understanding of how that played-out bitch was spoiling my vibe. Now a problem-free situation was showing signs of trouble just because of her existence in the distance.

Lucky for me, I had all the other principles of pimp procedure in place, so I didn't lose my hoes. But you better believe that situation opened my eyes in a major way, and I learned from it.

No matter what a hater does, you must keep it pushin' with your professional mission. Because the universe feeds whatever you focus your mind on, and then those things will grow in unpredictable ways. If you're not careful, you'll end up putting yourself in the exact position the hater wants to see you in; away from doing whatever makes your life better than theirs.

So, a player hater is never worthy of a player's attention. You do what you do and let them do what they do. Stay on your toes so they can't catch you slippin', and enjoy your own lane. That way they'll have to come out of hiding to get at you and you'll see them coming.

Don't taunt the haters, and don't try to teach them any lessons about hating on you. To do these things would be choosing to lose in the long run, because you're in the Game to pimp hoes and get money. Your job is to stick to your script. Simple as that. So ignore the haters.

SNEAK PEEKS

AOB

BY MIKE ENEMIGO, DUTCH, & MANNY FRESH

If you're feelin' Manny Fresh's Ism, check out his new series, *AOB*, which is based on actual events! Produced by Mike Enemigo and street-lit legend Dutch, you know it's a banger. Peep the sneak peek below, and be sure to snatch you a copy at thecellblock.net or Amazon.

PROLOGUE

Rosa's whole body tensed as she banged two fingers in and out of her pussy according to Manny's instruction. She was right at the verge of reaching her peak for the second time as he growled into the phone, driving her over the edge into another climax.

The bass in his voice sent invisible vibrations throughout her entire body in a way that was more than she could handle. She lost all control of herself and completely surrendered to the commands coming through the loudspeaker of her cell phone. Her hips humped hungrily against her hand as she came so hard a shiver was squeezed out from the strain of her pelvic muscles.

Riding the rhythm of her own touch, she moaned. "Ooooh, shit. I'm cummin' again!" Then she shot out a generous squirt.

When the last wave of her inner euphoria had finally passed, she caught her breath and marveled at how this mysterious man could so effectively seduce her using nothing more than his words. He often talked her through the full spectrum of sexually satisfying herself, and he did it with an intensity that left her feeling as if it was his hands instead of hers that coaxed the explosions from between her legs.

They'd met one day online when Manny decided to randomly reach out to her and introduce himself. After a few days of sending messages back and forth, they exchanged phone numbers so they could talk directly. But he was in California while she was in Texas, and neither one of them were doing well financially, so meeting in person wasn't an option at the time.

However, the vibe between them was a strong one. Their talks were long, deep, and personal, with a lot of details they'd never normally share. They genuinely liked what they saw in the pics they exchanged, and Rosa seriously enjoyed the sound of the words Manny spoke, even though he left her lost when he'd drop hints about doing what she had to do in order to get where she needed to be. And her confusion seemed to always cause him to say no more.

Since the long-distance situation was all they had to work with, they made the most of it. But day-to-day life will always prove to be a distraction to his kind of arrangement, so in spite of how memorable their phone calls never failed to be, the frequency still faded over time, until they eventually went their separate ways.

And yet, an impression was made upon their future that neither of them would have ever imagined possible. The energy of their mutual attraction tied the threads of their existence together, so that at some point, their paths were bound to cross...

CHAPTER 1

JOINING FORCES

"There is a difference between wishing for a thing and being ready to receive it."

– Napoleon Hill

Two years later...

Maaan, this shit is crazy, Manny thought to himself as he drove down the street in his black Super Sport Impala on 22-inch rims with 12-inch speakers bangin' away in the trunk. *Here I am in Stockton on some square shit wit' a bitch I damn near went broke to get away from, and now, as soon as she say she got some weed, I come runnin' back to smoke wit' the bitch.*

He laughed at himself as he drove down Charter Way, being too real to excuse his own compromise even as he made the move. He planned to be in constant disapproval of his actions the whole time he blew blunts with the girl.

The square lifestyle just wasn't a good fit for him, even though he was endlessly plagued with being able to like the girls he met. But when dramatic episodes of jealousy and a possessive mentality started to crop up in his relationships, his only instinct was to leave.

I could love a bitch if love was all I was lookin' for, he thought to himself as he stopped at a red light.

But any further thought was cut short when his eyes suddenly caught sight of something that scrambled his senses. After a spilt second of initial shock, he was able to actually register what he was seeing. Walking toward him on the sidewalk was one of the most impressively built Mexican girls he'd ever seen. She was "thick" in the physically attractive sense of the word. Her hips hinted at what Manny was sure would be a very wide and round butt. There was no doubt that she could stop traffic if she tried with the almost see-through black leggings she was wearing.

While he sat through the changing of traffic lights captivated by her image, he got a better look at her face as she came close enough for him to make out more details. That's when he understood why his attention was so stuck in her direction.

"That's my bitch!" he said out loud to himself in recognition.

All at once, his thoughts raced to recall her name as it raced through memories of the pics in his cell phone that she used to send, and the details about herself that she used to share. *She did say she used to live in California and had a son who lived with her dad, along with other family in or around the Stockton area.*

Trying to think of what to say to her, he was also faced with the challenge of getting her attention from behind his dark tinted windows. On top of the dark tint, he was in the far-left lane away from the sidewalk, stuck in traffic with a row of cars between him and the girl whose name he'd forgotten, as she walked on by without knowing he was even there.

Life itself seemed to jump into fast-forward as Manny's options both multiplied and ran out at the same time. So as soon as the traffic light turned green, he made an extremely illegal U-turn against on-coming traffic. This caused a symphony of horns to shriek in protest at how close Manny came to crashing into other drivers.

The girl noticed his wild move and expected it to be a prelude to some sort of harassment, so she quickly followed a particular protocol by aiming her attention elsewhere, and making her way into a nearby corner store to avoid being caught by this madman who was beeping his horn and aggressively edging his car into the lane next to the curb where she was walking.

Manny's thoughts were all over the place as he excitedly tried to avoid the multi-car pile-up his movements threatened to cause. Being from the Bay Area, he had a certain kind of exposure that rang a specific bell in his mind when he saw how the girl reacted to the way he was trying to get close to her. But he couldn't land on any conclusions because he was still preoccupied with trying his best to remember as much as he could in hopes of making a successful introduction. Something clicked in him when he recognized the face that made him want to freeze this moment before it passed him by.

Everything about this moment revolved around the big-booty Latina girl his eyes were on at the time, so like a man who'd never heard of traffic laws, he pulled up next to her as she tried to get into the store. When she disappeared inside, he hit his hazard lights and hopped out right there in front of the store.

"Ey, lil mama!" he yelled urgently to be heard over the sounds of his music and the wail of horns beeping behind him.

She went inside the doorway of the store and peeked out a semi-safe position where she could hear with a reduced risk of being harmed. Seeing she was listening, Manny continued to call her out. "I bet you think I'm just another nigga you need to be runnin' from, but I know you! Look at my face for real. We used to chop it up on the phone back when you was in Texas a couple years ago! You don't remember me?

"Yo' mama name is Linda, just like my mama. We was trippin' on that. And you got a son named Tookie, right?" he said in a rush of relevant information.

Her expression was somewhere between surprised curiosity and suspicious confusion as she fought the impulse to ask who he was, but the accuracy of the facts he fired at her proved he was indeed someone who knew her.

Knowing he had her attention, Manny started talking as if his life depended on every word he spoke. "Yeah, you know just any-ol'-body ain't gonna pop up on point like that, huh? I can't remember yo' name, but we was rockin' and rollin' kinda tough for a minute. I'm not tryna come at you crazy, but we 'posed to be together, girl! Whatever you doin' out here need to be includin' me! I'ma yank up in this parkin' lot so the police don't get me for stoppin' traffic, but don't bounce on me! You should come check me out!"

He tossed a few more facts at her about herself and then jumped back behind the wheel to pull out of traffic. There was no time to make sure she was coming, but his mind was back to thinking again.

If she brings that ass around this corner to see what I'm talkin' 'bout, I got me one for sure! he thought as he slid his big Impala into an empty parking space. He wanted to be visible, so he only pulled in halfway in hopes of her peeking into the parking lot and seeing him easily.

But nobody came around the corner of the building at all.... At least, not at first.

A wave of willpower went out from him to cover the space between them and hold her in place. Slowly, her hesitation went away and she approached him cautiously.

Very carefully, Manny said, "I ain't tryna play you. We met online, and you was far away. Now you close, and I'm tryna bring that shit back. If you out here doin' what it look like you might be doin', then you know what I mean when I say you should choose. And if what we was on ain't no fake shit, then you know we really ain't got no choice anyway, right? We gotta make somethin' happen."

While the words were falling from his mouth, understanding became recollection, and a look of recognition came over her features. She took the last few steps up to where Manny stood, and without word or warning, hugged him like a long-lost friend.

They stood in that embrace for a while as the cars drove by. No one in the world would ever believe they'd just been witness to what destiny could do, but the drivers of those cars were in proximity to more of a miracle than any of them could ever imagine.

Then she broke the spell: "My name is Rosa. And you shouldn't jump out on a bitch like that unless you want her to think you out here kidnappin' hoes!"

They made their way back into the car and Manny took Rosa to her motel room not far away.

After inviting him inside, she was quick to point out which of the two beds it was OK to sit on. He took note of this but made no comment.

Her immediate plan was to roll a few blunts and smoke their way into whatever happened next, so she retrieved a large bag of Northern California buds she had stashed in the dresser drawer. Laying a few Swisher Sweets cigarillos out and breaking some of the skunky smelling marijuana down, she saw Manny must've had the same plan when he picked up the blunts to prepare them for rolling.

Their harmony seemed natural with a very noticeable level of comfort between them – like old lovers who needed no extra effort to find familiarity.

Rosa didn't say much, but her mind was going a mile a minute. She now remembered very well exactly who Manny was, as well as where he fit into her past. It all came flooding back as she replayed the episodes of him turning her on over the telephone back when that was all they had. Now she had somehow been blessed with the opportunity of having him for real, and she'd be damned if she didn't try him out.

"Well... I don't know how the hell we ended up here after all this time, but you may not want me when you know for sure what I'm out there doin'. I'm tryna get my baby some school clothes, bein' about my money. That's why I don't want you on that other bed, because it's the work bed," she said in an effort to be straightforward before her instincts told her to lie.

When she glanced at him to check his reaction, she was met with a strange smirk on his face. Being somewhat self-conscious about what she'd just shared, her natural response to his expression was one of embarrassment.

"Oh... You think that's funny, huh?" she mumbled in a self-defeated tone.

"Naw, what's funny is the fact that you thought I didn't already know. As soon as you told me which bed to sit on, it was obvious. I wasn't born yesterday."

"So, you're OK fuckin' with a ho?"

"As long as you ain't tryna make me a trick!"

She smiled at his matter-of-fact way of speaking. "No, no, never that. But how is this supposed to work, though? You wasn't talkin' no pimp shit on the phone."

"No, I wasn't. And you wasn't a ho back then, either, right?"

169

"That's true. So now you gonna just snap your fingers and become a pimp?"

The smile went away and he looked at her very seriously. "I'm from the Bay, bitch. I know how to be whatever you need me to be. Since you happen to be a ho, I guess I need to be a P. Ain't nothin' I can't handle."

Rosa got anxious when hearing the bite in his tone. "I'm just sayin'... I ain't thinkin' you stupid or nothin'. Just trying to keep shit real."

"Well, luckily I'm a real nigga then, because real niggas do real things, right? So, it's whatever as long as you know it ain't no sucka shit."

They sat quietly for a little while as Manny twisted up the first blunt and lit it. After he hit it and passed it back to her, she noticed the strange half-smile back on his lips again.

When he saw she was paying attention, he slowly spilled a little speech he'd thought up.

"Look, Rosa. You ain't gotta be able to always guess what I'ma do next. That keeps you honest. But you do need to know that I won't ever change up on you unless you try to play me. So just make sure you gonna be in it all the way if you decide to fuck with me.

"As long as I'm around, consider yourself spoken for in every way. This includes everything that comes with you or from you. As far as I'm concerned, it's all for me – unless you say no. If that's the case, I'll be on my way."

Rosa had to think about that, but she didn't think for too long. She reached her decision, passed Manny the blunt, and quietly got up to go to the bathroom without saying anything.

When the sounds of the shower came from behind the closed door, Manny began to roll up another blunt. He'd made his move, and he wasn't going to say anything else until she did something to let him know what his next words should be. About halfway through smoking the blunt, he heard the water shut off, followed by the sounds of Rosa moving around in the bathroom.

Now for the next move...

He knew that the general rule in this kind of situation should be to get the purse first and ass last, but he also knew from watching his uncles that the rules were based more on principles than procedures.

Just as he came to a conclusion about what he might do, Rosa came into the room. She wore nothing except the smell of her body spray as she walked over to where he sat. And when she stopped to stand naked in front of him, it was clear that she was offering him her greatest gift.

Manny had no doubts that Rosa's body must be her most prized possession, and there was absolutely no question about why this was the case. She had round, firm, medium-sized breasts, and a soft, smooth stomach that sloped down between gorgeously-rounded hips, into a shaved pussy nestled neatly at the place where her luscious thighs met.

Without a moment of hesitation, he snatched her by the arm and flung her down onto the bed. The excitement that showed on her face was the only reaction she had time to experience before he followed up his move by flipping her onto her belly.

He kissed his way up from her lower back around to her sides. The whole time he did this, he expertly worked one finger, then two inside of her from behind. This type of teasing continued until her pussy was soaking wet.

When Rosa had grabbed the weed from the dresser drawer, Manny had spotted an obscene amount of condoms in there as well, so he had grabbed one for just this kind of possibility.

After removing his pants quickly with his free hand, he rolled the condom into place, removed the fingers of his occupied hand, and replaced them with his long, hard dick.

He grabbed her by the hips and drove himself into her. She met him thrust for thrust with a greedy arch of her back that raised her ass to receive him. A moan escaped her mouth.

It seemed only to encourage him and he fucked her even harder, pumping his dick into her until she was ready to cum.

She could tell from his hoarse breathing that he was getting close to orgasm himself. He used his slim, powerfully chiseled body to beat his way into her from the back. Then, suddenly, her whole world spun and she came with a shudder that rippled through her whole frame. This triggered Manny into exploding seconds later, releasing a brief groan.

"That shit was... Wow!" she said after a moment.

When Manny's breathing relaxed, he braced his body above her with their faces now close together. "Yeah, bitch, but don't you go thinkin' I just fell for no pussy-poppin' technique. I'm gonna pimp for you, and you gonna ho for me. So get yo' lil sexy ass up and give me whatever money you got in here so I can feel good about the rest of what I'm about to do to you," he said against her cheek.

Her obedience was immediate, spurred into action by the anticipation of getting more of him. She returned to the bed with what he demanded, and he delivered what she desired until the next day. The only interruption they tolerated were smoke breaks.

CHAPTER 2

LOCKIN' IT IN
"I got a good heart... But this heart can get ugly..."
– DMX

Over the next week, Manny came by every day to smoke and talk with Rosa, but he never stayed long or got comfortable. He would text her a lot, and sometimes she would see his car from a distance, moving around in the area near her motel while she was working.

At first, he offered no instruction at all; just gave her a puzzled expression whenever she answered his questions about how her days were going. Then, one day, he went to her room early in the morning with two cups of coffee from the gas station, both loaded with so much flavored cream and sugar, they tasted like hot milkshakes.

Rosa was already awake, but far from expecting him so early. She was surprised to hear him pull up in front of her room, but like always, excited when she heard the music bangin' from his car.

She was still wearing boy shorts and a wife beater when she opened the door to let him in. He quickly handed her a cup of the super sweet coffee and went into his next move as she sipped it.

"Don't know what you up to, cutie, but it's time to change your plans. Pack up whatever you can't leave or throw away, and let's take this show to the next level!" he said enthusiastically before spinning back out to his car.

Rosa was left with no chance to respond. All she could do was collect her belongings. She didn't have much, just a few outfits and cosmetics. Her whole little world was barely enough to fill up a pillowcase. But rather than be sad about her reality, she was thrilled to think about how much her life was about to change, and she smiled when she looked around

173

the now empty motel room as she imagined what was yet to come.

The honk of Manny's horn brought her back to focus. She hurried outside to put her things into the back seat and climb into the car with him. They rode off into the rising sun as they set out on the rest of their adventure...

PRETTY GIRLS LOVE BAD BOYS

By Mike Enemigo & King Guru

Tired of the same, boring, cliché pen pal books that don't tell you what you really need to know? If so, this book is for you! Anything you need to know on the art of long and short distance seduction is included within these pages! Not only does it give you the science of attracting pen pals from websites, it also includes psychological profiles and instructions on how to seduce any woman you set your sights on! Includes interviews of women who have fallen in love with prisoners, bios for pen pal ads, pre-written love letters, romantic poems, love-song lyrics, jokes and much, much more! This book is the ultimate guide – a must-have for any prisoner who refuses to let prison walls affect their MAC'n.

Check out this sneak peek and be sure to order your copy from theellblock.net or Amazon today!

$$$$$

Women have three major psychological conflicts they deal with. These conflicts are so intense it forces them to adopt a dominant strategy to deal with them, and this strategy tends to become a part of their personality. How they deal with these conflicts dictates what turns them on and determines who they are attracted to. These three conflicts are Time, Sex, and Relationships.

TIME

Remember, along with a survival instinct, humans have evolved over hundreds of thousands of years to be a certain way. There are anomalies in any aspect of life, especially when dealing with people. But for the most part other than cultural differences, biological needs are consistent. One of those consistencies are that most people want to procreate another human in their image. The difference between men and women is that females have time constraints and we don't. After menopause, women can't conceive life. Since they know this, it becomes a factor they have to deal with daily.

SEX

In the world we live in, society's rules dictate different freedoms for different sexes. Where a man who has multiple sex partners is considered a stud, a woman who does the same is a slut. Let's take Rihanna for instance. What is the difference between Rihanna going through life falling in and out of love with different men and say, some like Drake? Nothing, yet, we see Drake as a man who enjoys life and Rihanna is called an industry hoe for the doing the same thing.

RELATIONSHIPS

There is a certain amount of pressure put on women by themselves and others for them to start a family. There are certain families that'll make them feel guilty for not getting married and having kids. This can become an issue when they'd rather dedicate their lives to a career. All this has to be taken into consideration while you're operating on your seduction.

$$$$$

Of course, I'm gonna give you the Game to overcome each line of defense, but you have to understand them before you can manipulate them. What I'm going to do now is break down their psychological make-up. While I'm explaining them to you, I will use certain terms that I coined specifically for this project. The terms are as follows:

RENTER/BUYER: Women who date/court multiple guys at once will be referred to as "Renters." Women who try to fix men are "Buyers."

LIAR/OWNER: "Liars" pretend sex or sexual thoughts don't happen. "Owners" see sex as insignificant and let it happen all the time.

SHREWD/DREAMER: "Shrewd" focus on their careers almost to the point of eliminating the dating aspect of their life. "Dreamers" sometimes don't even consider their careers when love is in question.

Understanding these dimensions of women is critical to MAC'n. If you can understand the thinking that is taking place in the minds of women regarding the conflicts of Time, Sex, and Relationships you will be a beast at communicating with the opposite sex.

$$$$$

"THE PLAYGIRL"

Personality profile: Renter/Liar/Dreamer

The Playgirl is like that sexy librarian we've all fantasized about. If you're not on your shit she'll slide right past you because she's quiet and good at camouflaging herself. She's an observer. She doesn't wear emotions on her sleeve and she tends to keep her personal life under wraps.

HER TECHNIQUES: Playgirls are just like MAC's. They're RENTERS, don't ever forget it. They'll keep three or four dudes on their call list at all times. The thing is, you need to over-stand the reason she does this is because her ideal man is unrealistic. She has to have several different guys to fulfill each one of her needs. If she was a BUYER she'd lock onto one guy, but she's not. Remember this and you'll stay one step ahead of the competition.

POINTS OF CONQUEST: Playgirls keep a cipher of men getting at them so you'll have to set yourself apart from them. Even if you can't stop thinking about fucking the shit out of her, don't let her see that side of you. Everyone else is already doing that. If you really want her to fall for you, you need to appear unpredictable as well as uninterested sexually.

"COCAINE"

Personality profile: Renter/Owner/Dreamer

We all know them females who live like there's no tomorrow. Some people call 'em "Rippers," others call them "Party Girls." I'ma call them "Cocaine." They're turnt up and have a way of always leaving you wanting more. Cocaine is a mixture of Renter, Owner, and Dreamer. Everything about her is loose and fun. The thing is, her energy is contagious so every man in her cipher is gonna be feeling everything that you're feeling about her. What this means is you're going to have to compete with a lot of other guys.

HER TECHNIQUES: Cocaine will fuck with a guy just because he's hot. Nevertheless, "hot" can mean many different things to her. Well dressed, well kept, confident, nice smile, nice abs, etc. This girl gets different things from different men, and loves the newness of the stimuli. She likes to try different men for their kissing styles, dick sizes, fashion, the list is endless.

POINTS OF CONQUEST: It's not hard to get Cocaine's attention. It's keeping it that's the challenge. Your best bet is to find out what her interests are. It may sound obvious, but most guys screw this up by asking interview style questions. Pay attention to her – she wears her life on her sleeve. She'll talk about or display things that mean something to her. Comment on it and relate to it and you'll rise above the competition.

"ROMANTIC VISIONARY"

Personality profile: Owner/Liar/Dreamer

For the Romantic Visionary, daydreaming about the perfect man is an old and favorite pastime. The potential of long-term relationships is the foundation of all of her goals and dreams.

HER TECHNIQUES: The Romantic Visionary is a Buyer. She looks for sexual gratification and emotional fulfillment from one man, not several. When she meets a guy who catches her interest, she immediately begins to size him up as a long-term partner.

POINTS OF CONQUEST: When you're seducing a Buyer it pays to be straightforward. Why? Because she either has a man, or she's looking for one. If she has a man, chances are he's lacking in one or two areas that (sexual/emotional) she's looking for in a man. The best thing for you is if her current man isn't measuring up to emotional needs. That's where your MAC'n really needs to excel.

"BONNIE (and CLYDE)"

Personality profile: Buyer/Owner/Dreamer

Nine times out of ten, Bonnie is beautiful, stylish and far from square. She keeps her hair and nails done and dresses in clothes that fit right. She does this because she's searching for a man and wants to be ready at all times.

HER TECHNIQUES: Bonnie is both, "old school" and "new school" with her views on gender roles. Old school in the fashion that she respects her man. She wants you to take care of her and lead her. But she's "new school" in the aspect of sex. She's not a nun. She's the type that'll hold a whole conversation with you while you're in the shower, yet again she'll only do this if she likes you.

POINTS OF CONQEST: Immediately after breaking the ice, ask her questions about her life, and relate with your own experiences. Keep a nice balance of give and take. Keep your focus on how she thinks and feels about the topic. Don't get caught in logical facts – her Dreamer side gets bored with that. Focus on what make her tick and show her what makes you tick. This appeals to her Buyer strategy of finding a guy that wants to get to know her over the long-run.

"SECRET LOVER"

Personality profile: Renter/Liar/Shrewd

The Secret Lover is a giver by nature. She wants to be the source of her man's happiness. But this can open her up to being taken advantage of so she's very selective when choosing what man to bestow her blessings on.

HER TECHNIQUES: The Secret Lover will fraternize with other men because she can relate to the masculine way of thinking. She hates drama and thinks most women are catty. This is why she meets a lot of men, and has a lot of guys chasing her. There is something about her mysterious personality that draws men in.

POINTS OF CONQUEST: The best way to approach a Renter is to make a comment on something in the environment. If you give her a compliment, make sure it's something unrelated to her body. Whereas you can tell a Buyer you love how her dress fits around her curves. A Renter would be very uncomfortable hearing this. Especially since she doesn't see herself as a sexual person in general – only with that special guy.

"FEMME FATALE"

Personality profile: Renter/Owner/Shrewd

The Femme Fatale is a Renter, Owner, Shrewd. This combination makes her a very confident, sexual, independent woman. She is a Diva, not in the dramatic sense, but in the sense that she is strong, sexy, and has a presence that intimidates most men. That's good news for any guy reading this. Simply understanding her and knowing how to handle her is massively attractive since she views most men as weak. Since she's so career orientated, she doesn't have time to baby guys, so a strong man will immediately stand out to her.

HER TECHNIQUES: Ms. Femme Fatale knows that working in a prison means she's surrounded by horny guys. Even her coworkers are chasing her. Yes, she enjoys the attention but she doesn't want guys to be on her "nuts." She's looking for a challenge.

POINTS OF CONQUEST: Don't step to her with a bunch of flashy talk and one-liners. She doesn't react to the "ra-ra." She wants a confident man, a real man. And she's been bred to sniff one out on call.

"THE SAGE"

Personality Profile: Buyer/Liar/Shrewd

One of the hardest females to crack is the Sage. She's extremely picky and cautious in her approach to dating. For most guys the time and effort it takes to seduce her is too overwhelming, yet the payoff for a convict totally outweighs all efforts. Especially since we have an abundance of time.

HER TECHNIQUES: The Sage looks for long-term potential. Not a boyfriend, per se, but a guy who is interested in her as a person. She has a Shrewd perspective on men, so she knows if she gives in too fast she'll devalue herself in your eyes. These ruins the chances of her gaining your devotion.

POINTS OF CONQUEST: When complimenting her, pick out something specific. Don't talk about body parts or how her jumpsuit fits on her ass. Give her a good compliment then quickly move to less romantic conversation before she gets uncomfortable. A direct, sincere compliment is a great way to open up a dialogue.

"THE MILLENNIAL"

Personality profile: Buyer/Owner/Shrewd

The Millennial might have a boyfriend, but for the most part she's not clingy and is open to having casual fun. If she's not in a relationship, she'll most likely have a few "friends" she's willing to sleep with. This is good news for you because she's usually willing to try new things.

HER TECHNIQUES: The Millennial is active, she's talkative and extremely social. All her clothes fit well, hugging all the important curves. Sex is a perk that comes with being "free," so she's open to sexy conversations and peeking at "packages."

POINTS OF CONQUEST: As an Owner, the millennial woman is interested in your potential as well as your level of confidence. The best way to convey both is by being direct and honest in your approach. She likes knowing you chose her. Compliments work really well with this type of woman. But you gotta be smooth. Keep in mind she's already heard all the generic compliments from everyone else. You need to be unique in your approach. Don't forget to lock eyes with her every time you step to the plate.

$$$$$

If you're serious about your MAC'n, you really need to learn how to study your prey. It's literally impossible to use a "one-size-fits-all" method to seduce women in any type environment. You're going to have to get to know them as individuals and learn their motivations. They all have them.

You certainly can have some success treating all women the same, but you'll always have blind spots and this means you'll miss out on some opportunities. By tailoring your game to different types of women and having a flexible approach, you'll be in a position to maximize your efforts.

A woman is a woman whether she's a nurse, a parole agent or kitchen staff. Too many convicts forget this because of the line that has been drawn between us and them. I'm here to let you know that line is imaginary. It doesn't exist. Any female can be cracked, regardless of her profession, as long as you got the right game.

HOW TO HUSTLE & WIN: SEX, MONEY, MURDER EDITION

BY MIKE ENEMIGO & KING GURU

This is the grittiest underground self-help manual for the 21st Century Street entrepreneur in print. This book is for the block bleeders and breadwinners who get it how they live. In this book, King Guru takes the reader through the ghettos of Sacramento, the housing projects of Chattanooga, and the beaches and slums of Tampa Bay and the U.S. Virgin Islands. It's a mandatory read for anyone actively connected to the streets! Check out this sneak peek, and be sure to order your copy from thecellblock.net or Amazon today!

EMOTIONAL MANIPULATORS

"Keep ya' enemies close, nigga, watch yo' friends..."
– 2 Pac

Emotional: appealing to or arousing emotion
Manipulator: to influence with intent to deceive

As you navigate through life, especially in the Game, you'll quickly find out that a large portion of your problems will manifest from the individuals who are closest to you. There are too many of you who have the potential and the means to ball outta control, but your homies are what's keeping you down. Then there are those of you who have a nothin'-ass-bitch who is extremely passive aggressive, controlling and vindictive. And, just for the record, when I say, "nothin'-ass-bitch" I'm also referring to fuck-boys, too. Some of you females out there have the world at your fingertips but your so-called "man" is a loser and he's keeping you down.

Whether you're a hustler with broke-ass homies or you're in a relationship with an emotionally controlling person, chances are, you know it already. Yet, for reasons unbeknownst to you, you stay and stick around the toxic relationship no matter what losses you take. If this is the case, you may be in a relationship with an Emotional Manipulator. Don't get thrown off by the word "relationship" either. I'm using that word to describe any close association, affiliation and/or partnership; whether the link is money, sex or friendship, it's still a relationship.

Sometimes, even though you realize the relationship is the antithesis of profitable, you still maintain it out of a false sense of loyalty or even guilt. Well, I'm here to tell you that you need to look out for your own well-being. Fuck loyalty when that loyalty is dedicated to someone who uses it to their advantage. Fuck loyalty when that loyalty is used as a chain to keep you grounded. And fuck loyalty when the receiver is obviously, grossly not worthy of it!

You may or may not be involved with an Emotional Manipulator. If you aren't, that's great, keep it that way. If you feel like you may be, though, but you're not really sure, here are eight specific characteristics of one:

1. THERE IS NO USE IN TRYING TO BE HONEST WITH AN EMOTIONAL MANIPULATOR.

You make a statement and it will be turned around. Example: Your birthday went by and the person you're in said relationship with totally forgot it. The second you bring it up you'll most likely receive a reply that goes something like this; "I'm really angry that you would think that I would forget your birthday, I should have told you of the great personal stress I am facing at the moment – but you see, I just didn't want to bother you with it. You are right, I should have put all this pain to the side and focused on your birthday (don't be surprised if you see real tears at this point). Sorry." Even as you are hearing the words you get creeped out because you get the weird feeling that you both know the person is lying, but since they said the words, you're pretty much left with nothing more to say. Either that or you suddenly find yourself babysitting their false anxiety! Under all circumstances, if you feel this angle is being played – don't yield to it! Don't accept an apology that feels like bullshit. If it feels like bullshit, it probably is. The number one rule when dealing with an emotional blackmailer is to TRUST your gut. Trust your senses. Once an Emotional Manipulator finds a successful maneuver, it's added to their arsenal of weapons and it'll be utilized against you on a regular basis.

2. AN EMOTIONAL MANIPULATOR IS THE PICTURE OF A WILLING HELPER.

If you ask them to do something they will almost always agree. That is if they didn't volunteer to do it first. Then when you say, "Okay, thanks" – they'll make a bunch of heavy sighs, or other nonverbal signs that let you know they don't really want to do whatever said thing happens to be. When you tell them it doesn't seem like they want to do whatever

– they will turn it around and try to make it seem like OF COURSE they wanted to, and how unreasonable you are. This is a form of crazy making – which is something Emotional Manipulators are very good at. The second most important rule when dealing with Emotional Manipulators is whenever they agree to do anything, hold them to it! Don't buy into their sighs and subtleties. If they don't want to do it, make them tell you in words, or just ignore the sighs and go on with your business.

3. CRAZY MAKING: SAYING ONE THING AND LATER ASSURING YOU THEY DIDN'T SAY IT.

If you find yourself in a relationship where you figure you should start keeping a log of what's been said because you're beginning to question your own sanity – you are experiencing emotional manipulation. An Emotional Manipulator is an expert in turning things around, rationalizing, justifying and explaining things away. They can lie so smoothly that you can sit there looking at a blank screen and they'll swear there's something there. And what's so cold about it is that they'll argue so persuasively that you begin to doubt your very own senses. Over a period of time, this becomes so insidious and eroding that it can actually alter your sense of reality. WARNING: Emotional manipulation is very dangerous! It is very disconcerting for an Emotional Manipulator. If you start carrying around a pad of paper and a pen and taking notes during conversations, feel free to let them know you're just feeling so "forgetful" these days that you want to record what they talk about to make sure you don't miss anything. The damndest thing about this is that having to do something like this is a clear sign that you should seriously consider removing yourself from any type of relationship with this individual. If you've gotten to the point where you're carrying around a notebook to safeguard yourself from this person's bullshit, then it just can't be worth it.

4. GUILT: EMOTIONAL MANIPULATORS ARE EXCELLENT GUILT MONGERS.

They can make you feel guilty for speaking up or not speaking up, for being emotional or not being emotional enough, for giving and caring, or for not giving and caring enough. Anything is fair Game and open to guilt with an Emotional Manipulator. Emotional Manipulators seldom express their needs or desires openly – they get what they want through emotional manipulation. Guilt is not the only form of this but it is a potent one. Most of us are pretty conditioned to do whatever is necessary to reduce our feelings of guilt. Another powerful emotion that is used is sympathy. An Emotional Manipulator is a great victim. They inspire a profound sense of needing to support, care for and nurture. Emotional Manipulators seldom fight their own fights or do their own dirty work. The crazy thing is that when you do it for them (which they will never ask you to directly), they may just run around and say they certainly didn't want or expect you to do anything! Try to make a point of not fighting other people's battles, or doing their dirty work for them. A great line is, "I have every confidence in your ability to work this out on your own" – check out the response and note the bullshit meter kick into high gear.

5. EMOTIONAL MANIPULATORS FIGHT DIRTY.

They don't deal with things directly. They will talk behind your back and eventually put others in a position to tell you what they don't want to tell you themselves. They are passive aggressive, meaning they find subtle ways of letting you know they are not happy with your actions. They'll tell you what they think you want to hear, then do some backwards shit to undermine it. Example: "Of course I want you to go back to school, honey, and you know I got your back." Then exam night comes and you're cramming for the next day and suddenly a groups of homies show up, the kids are crying, the TV is blasting and the dog needs walking, all the while "Sweetie" is sitting on his or her ass looking at you like there's nothing wrong. And if you call 'em on it you might hear something like, "Well, you can't expect life to just stop because you have an exam, can you, honey?"

6. IF YOU HAVE A HEADACHE, THE EMOTIONAL MANIPULATOR WILL HAVE A BRAIN TUMOR!

No matter what your situation is, the Emotional Manipulator has probably been there or is there now – only ten times worse! It's hard after a period of time to feel emotionally connected to an Emotional Manipulator because they have a way of derailing your topic of conversation and putting the spotlight back on themselves. If you call them on this behavior they will likely become deeply wounded or very petulant and call you selfish, or claim that it's you who are always trying to have the spotlight. The thing is that even though you know this is not the case, you are now left with the impossible task of proving it. Don't even waste your time – just walk away!

7. EMOTIONAL MANIPULATORS SOMEHOW HAVE THE ABILITY TO IMPACT THE EMOTIONAL CLIMATE OF ALL THOSE AROUND THEM.

When an Emotional Manipulator is sad or angry, the very room vibrates with it; it brings a deep instinctual response to find some way to equalize the emotional climate and the quickest way is by making the Emotional Manipulator feel better – fixing whatever it is that's wrong with them or their situation. Stick with this type of loser for too long, and you will be so deep in the shit and codependent that you'll forget you've got your own needs, let alone that you have just as much right to have your needs met.

8. EMOTIONAL MANIPULATORS HAVE NO SENSE OF ACCOUNTABILITY.

They take no responsibility for themselves or their behavior – it is always about what everyone else has "done to them." One of the easiest ways to spot a damn Emotional Manipulator is that they often attempt to establish intimacy through the early sharing of deeply personal information that is meant to make you feel sorry for them. Initially you may perceive this type of person as very sensitive, emotionally open and maybe even a little vulnerable. Believe me when I say that an Emotional Manipulator is about as vulnerable as a rabid pit bull, and there will always be a problem or an error or a crisis to overcome.

This is only one type of obstacle that you may or may not have to deal with in your distant future. Keep an eye out for these types of people because they come in many shapes and sizes.

As a precaution, you must at all cost eliminate any weakness from your cipher. The Game don't play, fam. Someone like this is a cancer to your ultimate mission in life.

AFTERTHOUGHT: Who needs enemies when you got friends like this?

THE CELL BLOCK

BOOK SUMMARIES

MIKE ENEMIGO is the new prison/street art sensation who has written and published several books. He is inspired by emotion; hope; pain; dreams and nightmares. He physically lives somewhere in a California prison cell where he works relentlessly creating his next piece. His mind and soul are elsewhere; seeing, studying, learning, and drawing inspiration to tear down suppressive walls and inspire the culture by pushing artistic boundaries.

THE CELL BLOCK is an independent multimedia company with the objective of accurately conveying the prison/street experience with the credibility and honesty that only one who has lived it can deliver, through literature and other arts, and to entertain and enlighten while doing so. Everything published by The Cell Block has been created by a prisoner, while in a prison cell.

THE BEST RESOURCE DIRECTORY FOR PRISONERS, $17.95 & $5.00 S/H: This book has over 1,450 resources for prisoners! Includes: Pen-Pal Companies! Non-Nude Photo Sellers! Free Books and Other Publications! Legal Assistance! Prisoner Advocates! Prisoner Assistants! Correspondence Education! Money-Making Opportunities! Resources for Prison Writers, Poets, Artists! And much, much more! Anything you can think of doing from your prison cell, this book contains the resources to do it!

A GUIDE TO RELAPSE PREVENTION FOR PRISONERS, $15.00 & $5.00 S//H: This book provides the information and guidance that can make a real difference in the preparation of a comprehensive relapse prevention plan. Discover how to meet the parole board's expectation using these proven and practical principles. Included is a blank template and sample relapse prevention plan to assist in your preparation.

CONSPIRACY THEORY, $12.00 & $4.00 S/H: Kokain is an upcoming rapper trying to make a name for himself in the Sacramento, CA underground scene, and Nicki is his girlfriend. One night, in October, Nicki's brother, along with her brother's best friend, go to rob a house of its $100,000 marijuana crop. It goes wrong; shots are fired and a man is killed. Later, as investigators begin closing in on Nicki's brother and his friend, they, along with the help of a few others, create a way to make Kokain take the fall .... The conspiracy begins.

THEE ENEMY OF THE STATE (SPECIAL EDITION), $9.99 & $4.00 S/H: Experience the inspirational journey of a kid who was introduced to the art of rapping in 1993, struggled between his dream of becoming a professional rapper and the reality of the streets, and was finally offered a recording deal in 1999, only to be arrested minutes later and eventually sentenced to life in prison for murder... However, despite his harsh reality, he dedicated himself to hip-hop once again, and with resilience and determination, he sets out to prove he may just be one of the dopest rhyme writers/spitters ever .... At this point, it becomes deeper than rap .... Welcome to a preview of the greatest story you never heard.

LOST ANGELS: $15.00 & $5.00: David Rodrigo was a child who belonged to no world; rejected for his mixed heritage by most of his family and raised by an outcast uncle in the mean streets of East L.A. Chance cast him into a far darker and more devious pit of intrigue that stretched from the barest gutters to the halls of power in the great city. Now, to survive the clash of lethal forces arrayed about him, and to protect those he loves, he has only two allies; his quick wits, and the flashing blade that earned young David the street name, Viper.

LOYALTY AND BETRAYAL DELUXE EDITION, $19.99 & $7.00 S/H: Chunky was an associate of and soldier for the notorious Mexican Mafia -- La Eme. That is, of course, until he was betrayed by those, he was most loyal to. Then he vowed to become their worst enemy. And though they've attempted to kill him numerous times, he still to this day is running around making a mockery of their organization .... This is the story of how it all began.

MONEY IZ THE MOTIVE: SPECIAL 2-IN-1 EDITION, $19.99 & $7.00 S/H: Like most kids growing up in the hood, Kano has a dream of going from rags to riches. But when his plan to get fast money by robbing the local "mom and pop" shop goes wrong, he quickly finds himself sentenced to serious prison time. Follow Kano as he is schooled to the ways of the game by some of the most respected OGs whoever did it; then is set free and given the resources to put his schooling into action and build the ultimate hood empire...

DEVILS & DEMONS, $15.00 & $5.00 S/H: When Talton leaves the West Coast to set up shop in Florida he meets the female version of himself: A drug dealing murderess with psychological issues. A whirlwind of sex, money and murder inevitably ensues and Talton finds himself on the run from the law with nowhere to turn to. When his team from home finds out he's in trouble, they get on a plane heading south...

DEVILS & DEMONS: PART 2 $15.00 & $5.00 S/H:

The Game is bitter-sweet for Talton, aka Gangsta. The same West Coast Clique who came to his aid ended up putting bullets into the chest of the woman he had fallen in love with. After leaving his ride or die in a puddle of her own blood, Talton finds himself on a flight back to Oak Park, the neighborhood where it all started...

The is the second installment of the Devils & Demons series. Once again, publishing boss Mike Enemigo and street-lit legend and screenwriter Kwame "Dutch" Teague have collaborated with The Cell Block's very own hitmaker, King Guru, to bring you this urban saga that promises to have you turning pages till your fingers bleed!

DEVILS & DEMONS: PART 3 $15.00 & $5.00 S/H:

Talton is on the road to retribution for the murder of the love of his life. Dante and his crew of killers are on a path of no return. This urban classic is based on real-life West Coast underworld politics. See what happens when a group of YG's find themselves in the midst of real underworld demons...

This is the third installment of the Devils & Demons series. Once again, publishing boss Mike Enemigo and street-lit legend and screenwriter Kwame "Dutch" Teague have collaborated with The Cell Block's very own hitmaker, King Guru, to bring you this urban saga that promises to have you turning pages till your fingers bleed!

DEVILS & DEMONS: PART 4 $15.00 & $5.00 S/H:
After waking up from a coma, Alize has locked herself away from the rest of the world. When her sister Brittany and their friend finally take her on a girl's night out, she meets Luck – a drug dealing womanizer. Things get complicated when the Columbian sisters who were with B.A. when he killed Mike in the first book of this series slide into the picture; it triggers a psychotic breakdown in the murderess known as Ze. Follow your favorite Devil as she explodes in her unpredictable actions of rage! This is the fourth book in the Devils & Demons series, but it can also be read as book two.

THE ART & POWER OF LETTER WRITING FOR PRISONERS: DELUXE EDITION $19.99 & $7.00 S/H: When locked inside a prison cell, being able to write well is the most powerful skill you can have! Learn how to increase your power by writing high-quality personal and formal letters! Includes letter templates, pen-pal website strategies, punctuation guide and more!

THE PRISON MANUAL: $24.99 & $7.00 S/H: The Prison Manual is your all-in-one book on how to not only survive the rough terrain of the American prison system, but use it to your advantage so you can THRIVE from it! How to Use Your Prison Time to YOUR Advantage; How to Write Letters that Will Give You Maximum Effectiveness; Workout and Physical Health Secrets that Will Keep You as FIT as Possible; The Psychological impact of incarceration and How to Maintain Your MAXIMUM Level of Mental Health; Prison Art

Techniques; Fulfilling Food Recipes; Parole Preparation Strategies and much, MUCH more!

GET OUT, STAY OUT!, $16.95 & $5.00 S/H: This book should be in the hands of everyone in a prison cell. It reveals a challenging but clear course for overcoming the obstacles that stand between prisoners and their freedom. For those behind bars, one goal outshines all others: GETTING OUT! After being released, that goal then shifts to STAYING OUT! This book will help prisoners do both. It has been masterfully constructed into five parts that will help prisoners maximize focus while they strive to accomplish whichever goal is at hand.

MOB$TAR MONEY, $12.00 & $4.00 S/H: After Trey's mother is sent to prison for 75 years to life, he and his little brother are moved from their home in Sacramento, California, to his grandmother's house in Stockton, California where he is forced to find his way in life and become a man on his own in the city's grimy streets. One day, on his way home from the local corner store, Trey has a rough encounter with the neighborhood bully. Luckily, that's when Tyson, a member of the MOBTAR, a local "get money" gang comes to his aid. The two kids quickly become friends, and it doesn't take long before Trey is embraced into the notorious MOB$TAR money gang, which opens the door to an adventure full of sex, money, murder and mayhem that will change his life forever... You will never guess how this story ends!

BLOCK MONEY, $12.00 & $4.00 S/H: Beast, a young thug from the grimy streets of central Stockton,

California lives The Block; breathes The Block; and has committed himself to bleed The Block for all it's worth until his very last breath. Then, one day, he meets Nadia; a stripper at the local club who piques his curiosity with her beauty, quick-witted intellect and rider qualities. The problem? She has a man – Esco – a local kingpin with money and power. It doesn't take long, however, before a devious plot is hatched to pull off a heist worth an indeterminable amount of money. Following the acts of treachery, deception and betrayal are twists and turns and a bloody war that will leave you speechless!

HOW TO HUSTLE AND WIN: SEX, MONEY, MURDER EDITION $15.00 & $5.00 S/H: How To Hu$tle and Win: Sex, Money, Murder edition is the grittiest, underground self-help manual for the 21st century street entrepreneur in print. Never has there been such a book written for today's gangsters, goons and go-getters. This self-help handbook is an absolute must-have for anyone who is actively connected to the streets.

RAW LAW: Your Rights, & How to Sue When They are Violated! $15.00 & $5.00 S/H: Raw Law For Prisoners is a clear and concise guide for prisoners and their advocates to understanding civil rights laws guaranteed to prisoners under the US Constitution, and how to successfully file a lawsuit when those rights have been violated! From initial complaint to trial, this book will take you through the entire process, step by step, in simple, easy-to-understand terms. Also included are several examples where prisoners have sued prison officials successfully, resulting in changes of unjust rules and regulations and recourse for rights violations, oftentimes resulting in rewards of thousands, even millions of dollars in damages! If you feel your rights have been violated, don't lash out at guards, which is usually ineffective and only makes matters worse. Instead, defend yourself successfully by using the legal system, and getting the power of the courts on your side!

HOW TO WRITE URBAN BOOKS FOR MONEY & FAME: $16.95 & $5.00 S/H: Inside this book you will learn the true story of how Mike Enemigo and King Guru have received money and fame from inside their prison cells by writing urban books; the secrets to writing hood classics so you, too, can be caked up and famous; proper punctuation using hood examples; and resources you can use to achieve your money motivated ambitions! If you're a prisoner who want to write urban novels for money and fame, this must-have manual will give you all the game!

PRETTY GIRLS LOVE BAD BOYS: An Inmate's Guide to Getting Girls: $15.00 & $5.00 S/H: Tired of the same, boring, cliché pen pal books that don't tell you what you really need to know? If so, this book is for you! Anything you need to know on the art of long and short distance seduction is included within these pages! Not only does it give you the science of attracting pen pals from websites, it also includes psychological profiles and instructions on how to seduce any woman you set your sights on! Includes interviews of women who have fallen in love with prisoners, bios for pen pal ads, pre-written love letters, romantic poems, love-song lyrics, jokes and much, much more! This book is the ultimate guide – a must-have for any prisoner who refuses to let prison walls affect their MAC'n.

THE LADIES WHO LOVE PRISONERS, $15.00 & $5.00 S/H: New Special Report reveals the secrets of real women who have fallen in love with prisoners, regardless of crime, sentence, or location. This info will give you a HUGE advantage in getting girls from prison.

GET OUT, GET RICH: HOW TO GET PAID LEGALLY WHEN YOU GET OUT OF PRISON!, $16.95 & $5.00 S/H: Many of you are incarcerated for a money-motivated crime. But w/ today's tech & opportunities, not only is the crime-for-money risk/reward ratio not strategically wise, it's not even necessary. You can earn much more money by partaking in anyone of the easy, legal hustles explained in this book, regardless of your record. Help yourself earn an honest income so you can not only make a lot of money, but say good-bye to penitentiary chances and prison forever! (Note: Many things in this book can even he done from inside prison.) (ALSO PUBLISHED AS HOOD MILLIONAIRE: HOW TO HUSTLE AND WIN LEGALLY!)

THE MILLIONAIRE PRISONER: SPECIAL 2-IN-1 EDITION, $24.99 & $7.00 S/H: Why wait until you get out of prison to achieve your dreams? Here's a blueprint that you can use to become successful! The Millionaire Prisoner is your complete reference to overcoming any obstacle in prison. You won't be able to put it down! With this book you will discover the secrets to: Making money from your cell! Obtain FREE money for correspondence courses! Become an expert on any topic! Develop the habits of the rich! Network with celebrities! Set up your own website! Market your products, ideas and services! Successfully use prison pen pal websites! All of this and much, much more! This book has enabled thousands of prisoners to succeed and it will show you the way also!

THE MILLIONAIRE PRISONER 3: SUCCESS UNIVERSITY, $16.95 & $5 S/H: Why wait until you get out of prison to achieve your dreams? Here's a new-look blueprint that you can use to be successful! The Millionaire Prisoner 3 contains advanced strategies to overcoming any obstacle in prison. You won't be able to put it down!

THE CEO MANUAL: HOW TO START A BUSINESS WHEN YOU GET OUT OF PRISON, $16.95 & $5.00 S/H: $16.95 & $5 S/H: This new book will teach you the simplest way to start your own business when you get out of prison. Includes: Start-up Steps! The Secrets to Pulling Money from Investors! How to Manage People Effectively! How To Legally Protect Your Assets from "them"! Hundreds of resources to get you started, including a list of 'loan friendly" banks! (ALSO PUBLISHED AS CEO MANUAL: START A BUSINESS, BE A BOSS!)

THE MONEY MANUAL: UNDERGROUND CASH SECRETS EXPOSED! 16.95 & $5.00 S/H: Becoming a millionaire is equal parts what you make, and what you don't spend-- AKA save. All Millionaires and Billionaires have mastered the art of not only making money, but keeping the money they make (remember Donald Trump's tax maneuvers?), as well as establishing credit so that they are loaned money by banks and trusted with money from investors: AKA OPM -- other people's money. And did you know there are millionaires and billionaires just waiting to GIVE money away? It's true!

These are all very-little known secrets 'they" don't want YOU to know about, but that I'm exposing in my new book!

OJ'S LIFE BEHIND BARS, $15.00 & $5 S/H: In 1994, Heisman Trophy winner and NFL superstar OJ Simpson was arrested for the brutal murder of his ex-wife Nicole Brown-Simpson and her friend Ron Goldman. In 1995, after the "trial of the century," he was acquitted of both murders, though most of the world believes he did it. In 2007 OJ was again arrested, but this time in Las Vegas, for armed robbery and kidnapping. On October 3, 2008 he was found guilty sentenced to 33 years and was sent to Lovelock Correctional Facility, in Lovelock, Nevada. There he met inmate-author Vernon Nelson. Vernon was granted a true, insider's perspective into the mind and life of one of the country's most notorious men; one that has never provided...until now.

BMF, $18.99 & $5 S/H: The Black Mafia Family – was a drug organization headed by brothers Demetrius "Big Meech" Flenory and Terry "Southwest T" Flenory. Rising up from the shadows of Detroit's underbelly, they created a cross-country cocaine network, becoming two of the wealthiest, most dangerously sophisticated drug traffickers the United States has ever seen.

BLACK DYNASTY, $15.00 & $5 S/H: After their parents are murdered in cold blood, the Black siblings are left to fend for themselves in the unforgiving streets. But when the oldest brother, Lorenzo, is introduced to his deceased father's drug connection, he is given the opportunity of a lifetime to put his family back on top.

JAILHOUSE PUBLISHING: $24.99 & $7 S/H: In 2010, after flirting with the idea for two years, Mike

Enemigo started writing his first book. In 2014, he officially launched his publishing company, The Cell Block, with the release of five books. Of course, with no mentor(s), how-to guides, or any real resources, he was met with failure after failure as he tried to navigate the treacherous goal of publishing books from his prison cell. However, he was determined to make it. He was determined to figure it out and he refused to quit. In Mike's new book, Jailhouse Publishing for Money, Power, and Fame, he breaks down all his jailhouse publishing secrets and strategies, so you can do all he's done, but without the trials and tribulations he's had to go through...

KITTY KAT, ADULT ENTERTAINMENT RESOURCE BOOK, $24.99 & $7.00 S/H: This book is jam packed with hundreds of sexy non nude photos including photo spreads. The book contains the complete info on sexy photo sellers, hot magazines, page turning bookstore, sections on strip clubs, porn stars, alluring models, thought provoking stories and must-see movies.

PRISON LEGAL GUIDE, $24.99 & $7.00 S/H: The laws of the U.S. Judicial system are complex, complicated, and always growing and changing. Many prisoners spend days on end digging through its intricacies. Pile on top of the legal code the rules and regulations of a correctional facility, and you can see how high the deck is being stacked against you. Correct legal information is the key to your survival when you have run afoul of the system (or it is running afoul of you). Whether you are an accomplished jailhouse lawyer helping newbies learn the ropes, an old head fighting bare-knuckle for your rights in the courts, or a hustler just looking to beat the latest write-up – this book has something for you!

PRISON HEALTH HANDBOOK, $19.99 & $7.00 S/H: The Prison Health Handbook is your one-stop go-to source for information on how to maintain your best health while inside the American prison system. Filled with information, tips, and secrets from doctors, gurus, and other experts, this book will educate you on such things as proper workout and exercise regimens; yoga benefits for prisoners; how to meditate effectively; pain management tips; sensible dieting solutions; nutritional knowledge; an understanding of various cancers, diabetes, hepatitis, and other diseases all too common in prison; how to effectively deal with mental health issues such as stress, PTSD, anxiety, and depression; a list of things your doctors DON'T want YOU to know; and much, much more!

All books are available on Amazon and thecellblock.net website. Prices may differ between Amazon and our website.

You can also order by sending a money order or institutional check to:

The Cell Block
PO Box 1025
Rancho Cordova, CA 95741

Made in the USA
Las Vegas, NV
26 September 2023